Dedicated to the suffragettes, pioneers and free thinkers
who make life worth living

Acknowledgements

I'd like to thank everybody who has helped and contributed to this work. In particular, the living relatives of Alice G. Colman: grandson Robert Colman and his wife Ruth, for providing vital family information on Alice, and giving their blessing to this project; and Alice's great granddaughters, Lorna Pullman and Shirley King, for providing photographs and putting me in touch with Robert.

To my partner Catherine McMahon, for endless proof-readings, early edits and continued love and support.

Table of Contents

Introduction

....

*"Life is like art done in chalk, beautiful but
temporary... enjoy it while you can."*

....

Anon

Today the inhabitants of London are surrounded by an endless
vista of bricks and mortar; they would be forgiven for forgetting
that this pavemented valley was once a wild and primitive place.
Historically, Londoners have always had a close connection
with chalk – the city was built on it. Peel away the pavements
and the cobblestones, dig down beyond the gravel and the clay
layers, keep digging and still digging downwards, and you will
come to the chalk layer. Six hundred and fifty five feet thick,
and covering the whole of London, the city's chalk was created
millions of years ago by billions and billions of tiny shellfish
when London sat at the bottom of a shallow tropical sea.

It's the same chalk that forms the white cliffs of Dover, the
South Downs, the Chilterns and almost the whole of southern
Britain. The small hill on which the Queen's residency at
Windsor Castle stands is made of solid chalk.

In this dark and damp corner of Europe, on this most
unlikely of islands and in this city built on chalk, London
became the centre of a street art culture, the likes of which had
never been seen before.

The magic quality of chalk

To stumble upon an unguarded piece of pavement art, produced by an unknown artist in a place where you least expect it, can itself be a magical experience. It encapsulates the delicate nature of chalk and its ability to produce what looks like permanent art on the flagstones, only for the rain to come and wash it all away, leaving barely a trace.

We have always had a fascination with creating art from coloured earths; some of the most fascinating examples of prehistoric art we find chalked onto cave walls, shut off and hidden for thousands of years, passed down to us by a magic of accident rather than design.

It is thought that these drawings had some kind of storytelling or magical properties never meant for preservation. Like pavement art, they lived in the moment of their creation. Archaeologists have speculated over the nature of rock carvings and spiral designs, suggesting that they may have originated as magic markings – chalk lines drawn on the smooth trunks of fig mulberry trees, to cast spells, invoke spirits or mark out territorial boundaries.

In Britain, stories have persisted about chalk circles that were drawn around babies' cots to prevent them being stolen by fairies. The circles were drawn in a clockwise pattern and were accompanied by spells and incantations. Fairies were regarded as evil spirits who would maliciously steal and replace children with fairy babies, otherwise known as *changelings*.

In pagan religions these chalk circles were also known as *magic circles*. People believed spaces marked out on the ground would contain a special energy, and form a sacred space; providing a form of magical protection drawn in chalk or salt. The barrier was believed to be so fragile that leaving or passing through the circle would weaken or dispel it. This is where the phrase 'breaking the circle' comes from. Chalk pentagrams and symbols would also be drawn on the outside of the dwelling to ward off evil spirits – any maleficent entity trying to enter the circle would be detected immediately by the smudging of the chalk.

In England, some of the earliest examples of prehistoric 'public art' still exist, mainly carved into the chalk downs of the southern counties of Wiltshire and Dorset. The public nature of landscape art makes it clear that it was intended for a wide audience.

Giant drawings were created by cutting deep trenches into hillsides, revealing the underlying white chalk rock. The Cerne Abbas Giant and the Uffington White Horse are perfect examples of this prehistoric land graffiti.

The birth of pavement art

Pavement artists appeared on the streets of London when they became paved with stone rather than cobbles. This could have happened as early as the mid 1400s, when London's first pavement squares were being laid. Itinerant beggars scrawled 'begging letters' known as screevings on the stones – *'Can You Help Me Out'* was a favourite. *'I am Starving'* and other variations would appear with little or no artistry involved. Over a long period of time, the pavement artist evolved, and by the 1850s had chalked the words *'All My Own Work'* and *'Every Little Helps.'*

These street artists had their own particular pitches. The corners of fashionable squares and affluent neighbourhoods were considered ideal territory – Cockspur Street and opposite the restaurants on The Strand were favoured locales.

Many of these 'screevers' – as they had become known – were demoralised artists whose orthodox work had not prospered. Simeon Solomon was a highly respected Pre-Raphaelite painter who ended up as a pavement artist in Bayswater and died an alcoholic on the street. Others were homeless or unemployed, and saw an opportunity requiring only coloured chalks and a duster to conjure up a landscape or a portrait upon the stones. Some artists specialised in portraits of contemporary politicians, or sentimental scenes of landscapes; one artist painted religious scenes along Finchley Road, while in the Whitechapel Road another specialised in scenes of fire and burning houses. They satisfied the tastes of the London public by painting in the crudest and most garish tones.

By curious association, their works on the pavement directly mirrored the sky above the city. In *Highways and Byways of London*, Mrs E.T. Cook reported that the sky behind the 'artists lodging house in Drury Lane would often be robed in intense hues of orange, purple and crimsons', as if mimicking the colours of the pavement artist. George Orwell, in *Down and Out in Paris and London*, recalled the conversation of Bozo, whose pitch was close to Waterloo Bridge. He was walking with Orwell back to his lodgings in Lambeth, but was all the time looking up at the heavens. 'Say, will you look at Aldebaran! Look at the colour. Like a – great blood orange….Now and again I go out at night and watch meteors.' Bozo had engaged in correspondence with the Astronomer Royal on the subject of the sky above London, so that for a moment the city and the cosmos were intimately connected in the life of one wandering street artist.

As Oscar Wilde so brilliantly put it 'We are all in the gutter, but some of us are looking at the stars.'

Art of the flagstones

"The world worn squalid-looking men who may be seen in all parts of London, working on the pavement with their dirty bundle of chalks, and bits of leather, are unconsciously practising art in its primeval form.

"The earliest satirist and the earliest idealist both used this medium. The first artist born into the world probably made an ugly drawing of his enemy, or attempted a crude likeness of his lady love with a piece of charcoal or red chalk upon a smooth stone.

"Thousands of village Raphaels in past ages have made their evanescent sketches thus, sunk into oblivion without ever smelling paint or handling a marl-stick. The boy Giotto might have scratched his rude designs with perfect satisfaction to himself, and died a simple shepherd, had not Cimabue chanced to see him at work in the fields of Vespignano.

"Others as gifted as he, but to whom fate sent no Cimabue, may have lived, and dreamed, and died unknown."

— *Dundee Evening Telegraph, Tuesday 20 June 1899*

CHAPTER ONE

The Alice Colman story

The world's first female pavement artist

The late 1800s was the high watermark of British prosperity – London had become the largest metropolis the world had ever seen, and economic factors brought wealth from all parts of the Empire, making the modern port of London the world's richest trading centre. Victorian London was a tale of two cities, and with a populous of around six million; the minority rich rubbed shoulders with the masses of the poor. Ordinary people did whatever they could to 'make the both ends meet.'

Born in the Paddington district of London in 1874, Colman was christened Alice Geneviève Temple – the daughter of a somewhat obscure actor and playwright Noel Temple. Alice's birth certificate has never been found, so we cannot be absolutely certain of the date and place of her birth. The only indication of her father's name comes from Alice herself as she declared it on her first marriage certificate. The Colman family were never quite sure if Alice was adopted or even if Noel Temple was really her father or her father's stage name.

....

"The true pavement artist does not beg, we never hold our hand out and ask for money. Our transaction is a trade, if people go away happier for seeing our work, then they can show their appreciation if they wish."

....

Alice interviewed in the English Illustrated News for the article
Pavement Artists and their Work, October 1898

There can be no doubt that Noel Temple did exist.

A Noel Temple was mentioned in 1877, as he appeared in an Opera Comique production of Gilbert and Sullivan's *HMS Pinafore*, produced by the famous D'Oyle Carte Company. He also played the part of King Cobweb (surrounded by his attendant demons) for a pantomime production of *Cinderella* in 1884. He was mentioned again in an unnamed Royal English Opera production of 1885. Soon after, his theatrical career faded and his memory was lost to the endless sea of time.

Not much is known about Alice's early childhood, but the family oral history passed down the years claimed her mother was an opera singer who had a flirtation with a Spanish Count;

THE LADY PAVEMENT ARTIST.

Lady pavement artist – LONDON:WEEK-BY-WEEK,
Saturday 25 September 1893

Alice Geneviève Temple age 17, c.1890 (Colman family photo)

they got married and Alice was the result. The Count's family hotfooted it to England, the marriage was annulled and the Count and his family returned to Spain.

Naturally, there is always the tale of a lost fortune, and another story of an Italian Marquis and a large sum of money

3

put into a trust fund for Alice with a solicitor, who at some stage absconded with the money.

It is possible that Alice was born illegitimately and so would have been christened under a different name; this would explain the lack of a birth certificate. Whatever the truth, it's fair to say that Alice was abandoned to the charge of her grandmother at an early age. Interviewed in the Westminster Budget, on 8 December 1893, Alice revealed: "My father and mother were both in the theatrical profession, and early in life I was left to the charge of my grandmother, with whom I lived until I left school at the age of 14, when I obtained a situation as a clerk to a neighbouring butcher."

Alice's first love was the theatre, and in her teens she joined a touring theatre company. During the reign of Queen Victoria theatres flourished – the theatrical atmosphere was not restricted to certain classes of the society. The improvement in the transportation system resulted in 'the masses' attending the theatre; improved street lighting increased the safety of travelling at night. It was while performing with her troupe of players that Alice met husband and fellow performer, Robert Colman.

....

"Soon after I fell in love with a travelling acrobat; but my grandmother objecting to my marrying anyone connected with the profession followed by my parents, I was sent away to some friends residing a little distance from London. This, however, proved useless, and at the age of seventeen I was married and joined my husband in his performances."

....

Robert and his three brothers (Edward, Harry and James) had started a street acrobatic troupe, but he was also a talented artist and scenic painter for the local theatre.

Actress Alice Geneviève Temple (second from left) aged 17, c.1890
(Colman family photo)

After the customary courtship, Alice and Robert married at St Michael and All Angels Parish Church on the splendidly named Artesian Road, Kensington on Monday 30 November 1891. They were both living at number 3, Branston Street.

A street performer's life was not always a happy one – it could often be low paid and intermittent. Robert and his brothers – *The Jumping Jacks* – honed their skills on the streets of London, and were now good enough to join the local circus. Their act would have included classic tumbling and balancing routines, designed to delight and enchant the crowd. One of their specialities was the comic routine of jumping over eggs without breaking them. *The Jacks* were getting a good reputation as comic clowning acrobats, including a high wire routine that would prove fateful.

In the circus, they performed alongside speciality acts including ventriloquists, aerial acts, one-legged dancers, adagio acts, jugglers, magicians, cyclists and sword-swallowers; acts involving electricity, animal acts, slapstick sketches and illusionists.

In the late 19th century there were hundreds of circuses operating in Britain. Trick riding was the main attraction, but a variety of other acts, including acrobats, developed. There was even an aquatic circus were the circus ring was flooded with water.

Such was the popularity of circuses that many 19th century theatres also presented circus acts – you were as likely to see jugglers and aerial acts on a trip to the music hall as at a circus. Trapeze wires were strung from the roof of the Alhambra and other theatres, and trapeze and high wire artists performed

LONDON STREET ACROBATS

Street Acrobats: The Graphic Magazine, 1890

above the crowds sitting in the stalls. Even Drury Lane theatre had a circus ring so it could present equestrian acts.

Circuses were dangerous places (as were most Victorian places of work), and death or serious injury was a frequent visitor.

They had only been married for two years when tragedy unfolded at Branston Street; Alice was 19 years of age when her husband was brought home. A contemporary newspaper report described the scene:

"They carried him home from the circus ring on a stretcher; a pathetic Punchinello with the painted, scarlet smile that was the badge of his profession, mocking his agony. They broke the news to the white-faced, frightened girl who had met them at the door – his young bride. They told her of his fall from the trapeze swinging high above the sawdust ring. They told her he will never clown again..... Robert broke his back as he fell from the dizzy heights of the big top and became helplessly paralysed."

So tragedy came to the circus jester and his teenage wife. Day after day the man lay staring at the ceiling with hopeless eyes, unable to raise a finger to help his little family – a broken clown. The acrobatic dream castles they had planned tumbled about their ears and, as their scanty savings dwindled to a few shillings, poverty and hunger reared their ugly heads.

Looking back, Alice recalled: "I was very happy when I married, and my husband was the best husband in the world. We had saved quite a nice little nest egg in case anything happened, but we never thought that we would want it so soon. After my husband's accident I tried to get work, but could find nothing."

From that day their whole outlook changed. The young wife searched for work in vain; weary and sad at heart, she came home each night to her invalid husband and their baby crying for food. It was her baby's crying in hunger that steeled her to do what became a life-long career.

Before his accident, Robert had practiced pavement art as a sideline, and a way of earning an extra income. In desperation, she tried to sell Robert's sketches and drawings in the local shops, but without success. Alice thought about Robert's time on the street and had seen men drawing on the pavements: the idea struck her that *'what a man could do a woman could do equally well.'*

With starvation staring the family in the face, and the last few coins in her purse, she bought a pennyworth of coloured chalks. Then she found a quiet spot and, kneeling on the pavement, began to draw with trembling fingers: "With the last of our savings I bought some chalks, and in a nearby district where I was unknown, I drew my first sketches."

Alice knew no trade to which she could turn, and her only hobby before her marriage had been drawing. So, putting her pride in her pocket, she went to a district where she was not known, and drew her pavement pictures.

"I can still remember that terrible day," she recalled, many years later. "After my husband's accident it was only because our baby was crying that I plucked up sufficient courage to start, I shall never forget my first day. I felt that everyone was staring at me. Every time anyone stopped to look at my drawings I feared that I would be recognised. My fingers trembled so that I could hardly hold the chalk, but somehow I finished my picture and at the end of the day I came home with 3 shillings and tuppence* in my purse. How proud I was!"

*3 shillings and tuppence is equivalent to £20 today.

Alice created such a stir on her first day that a crowd soon gathered around her, but she was so fearful that she dare not even look up. Even the cab men stopped their horses in order to have a look at this unique spectacle. At last, having finished her tenth drawing, Mrs Colman plucked up sufficient courage to sit on a campstool and face her audience. Alice's first day was reported later in the Australian newspaper Albury Banner and Wodonga Express (Friday 16 April 1909):

"Doing it for a bet!" said one.

"Actress trying to advertise herself!" explained another.

And a butcher's boy, after carefully studying first the drawings and then the artist, inquired "Going to show anyfink at the Academy miss?"

She had earned three and tuppence – enough to keep the wolf from the door.

Her husband's life was in the balance for over a year. He began to mend slowly, until at last he was able to walk with help, but still he had to depend on his stout-hearted wife. Every day she went out with her coloured chalks, trying to earn a few shillings. "That feeling of fear soon wore off and I began to improve in the work," she admitted later.

It was early September 1893, and Alice's first drawing pitch was at Brook Green, Hammersmith. As a young girl, she had exhibited 'a marked talent' in the use of a pencil at school. She learnt the art of colouring from watching her husband Robert, as he painted scenery at the local theatre. Her first efforts at pavement art were a landscape and a dish of fishes – the standard fare of the London screever. The unusual sight of a woman at the work brought so many enquiries that, to use her own words, "I felt like jumping up and running away." After a time, she lost her nervousness, and found that the general public were invariably very kind.

....

"They treat me very nicely, and I have got accustomed to the open air; it suits my health."

....

Alice recalled that her first coin was not in connection with her work, but from an old gentleman who, preoccupied with his paper, stumbled over her, and gallantly accompanied his apology with a sixpence.

Alice's appearance on the streets of London caused quite a stir, and it wasn't long before the newspapers started to filter through the news of A Lady Pavement Artist. The Lloyds Weekly reported: "One day last week whilst riding through St. John's Wood, I noticed a crowd admiring as I thought a charwoman washing the flagstones in front of a garden gate, but I discovered that this was a female chalker 'screeving' on the flagstones. The press is making a fuss over this artistic novelty and no doubt in a day or two she will be "interviewed" by more than one member of it."

For Alice, working as a pavement artist was not that far removed from theatrical work; both required an element of live performance, and the public were often the screever's harshest critic. Alice travelled all over the south of England, and in all quarters of London. In the quiet streets of Kensington and St. John's Wood, she acquired regular patrons and was continually improving her art on a daily basis; from her curious vantage point, she was in a position to learn something about human nature – her living depended on it. She had become a landmark, a pleasant feature of the streetscape, and people were certainly none the worse for seeing her. Interviewed in *The Westminster Budget*, Alice explained:

....

"I was always very fond of drawing when at school, and took great interest in my husband's artistic work, so that when he became too ill to go out, and it became necessary for me to do something to keep the wolf from the door, I determined to try my own skill in producing pictures on the pavement.

"Accordingly having selected a 'pitch,' I commenced to reproduce some of the studies I had seen my husband execute. Several times, however, I had to give up in despair; but at last my efforts were crowned with success, and attracted a considerable amount of attention from passers-by, who liberally responded. Now that the great difficulty of commencement was over, I took kindly to the work, and think I can say, without self-flattery, that I have greatly improved."

....

THE LADY PAVEMENT ARTIST.

The latest phase of feminine enterprise is the appearance of a lady artist on the pavement. The phenomenon has moved Mr. Harry Furniss to send the accompanying sketch to *The Yorkshire Weekly Post.*

PRESS CUTTING – Yorkshire Weekly Post: Saturday 21 October 1893

Alice G Colman: The Lady Pavement Artist (1893) Illustrated by Lionel J Jones

Alice's income varied according to the weather – about 5 shillings per day (£28 today) would be a fair estimate. Of course, in wet weather and in winter her work would be at a standstill, and at these times she remained at home painting cards, and preparing chalks, all of which she manufactured herself.

Alice always downplayed her work, particularly in the light of male competition – in an effort to diffuse tensions she would write a chalk legend in perfect copperplate next to her art "This is the work of a woman of really no importance."

Considerable jealousy existed among her male competitors at the invasion of their territory by a woman, but it cannot be denied that Alice's work had a great deal of artistic merit. She would take all possible opportunity in the studying of nature, taking a special interest in sunset effects, in which she was beginning to excel, and fully justifying the remark she would write by the side of her drawings:

....

"Some people say this is not my own work. If they have any doubt about it, would they kindly ask me to produce a picture before them, instead of running away with the idea that this is 'one of the many impositions palmed off upon the public'?"

....

AT HOME.

Alice Colman's home (73, Latymer Road, Hammersmith) December 1893, Illustrated by Lionel J Jones

ART ON THE PAVEMENT.

The lady street-artist has made her appearance in Gray's Inn road, London. On Tuesday morning she took up a position, and speedily produced the customary red and yellow sunsets, half-cucumbers, eruptions of Vesuvius, the ship in a storm, and all the rest of the well-known designs. Later on two male artists of the same kind arrived to take possession of the pavement, and stood thunder-struck on finding that it was already occupied. The two male artists looked at the pictures, and one said to the other, "Well, I'm blest; it's come to this at last, 'as it?" "Yes," said the other, "it 'ave. They're drivin' us out of the Academy, and now they're drivin' us off the street as well. We'll 'ave to jine the unemployed." "Or go to the work'us," added the first. And they went away.

PRESS CUTTING: Sheffield Daily Telegraph – Thursday 12 October 1893

It was not uncommon for Alice to arrive at a favourite spot, only to find huge initials chalked there – if she disregarded them and started work, the owner of the initials would promptly put in an appearance and cause trouble. It was the men's way of objecting to the intrusion of a woman into their ranks.

The following year in 1894, it was estimated that there were at least 300 pavement artists – men and lads – earning a living drawing chalk pictures on the streets of London, and collecting pennies from the crowds that gathered. Oh yes, and one gentlewoman, Mrs. Colman, who was supporting herself, her children and her sick husband.

The Nottinghamshire Guardian reported: "If a lady, a pretty one, were bold enough to follow the example of the female chalker I saw, she could snap her fingers at the Royal Academy and the dealers, and make her fortune in a season."

Alice had become the talk of the town, and her story was reported in almost every newspaper across the land and even further afield. On the 7 January 1894, the New York Times reported that:

"Force of circumstances has driven an Englishwoman – one Mrs. Colman – to adopt the unusual occupation of pavement artist. She is probably the first gentlewoman to attempt this calling, which is one of the common street sights of London."

She remained the only English woman street 'screever,' to pick-up her living by applying coloured chalks to the pavement.

It was an important year for Alice – as her pavement art career was taking off, she celebrated the birth of her second child. Maud Dorothy was born on 13 March 1894. She was baptised just off Portobello Road at All Saints Church, Notting Hill on 3 April. Maude was Alice's second child – her first child, also called Alice, died of consumption (tuberculosis) when she was about five years of age.

		Parent's Name.				
When Baptised.	Child's Christian Name.	Christian.	Surname.	Abode.	Quality, Trade, or Profession.	By whom the Ceremony was performed.
1894 April 7th No.353	Maud Dorothy	Robert + alice	Colman	75 Latimer Rᵈ	artist	7. Davies

Page 40

BAPTISMS solemnized in the Parish of *S Clement Notting Hill* in the County of *London* in the Year 1894

Alice's daughter Maud Dorothy's baptism, 3 April 1894

Alice had six children in total but only two survived; Alice was the eldest, then Maud; Robert died a few weeks after being born, and little Ethel, who found a penny on the floor, picked it up, and popped it into her mouth. The copper penny got lodged in her oesophagus (windpipe) and gangrene set in, and she died soon after. Ethel's symptoms would have been minor – a cough now and again, but no gagging or anything like that; she would have had trouble swallowing, and after a few weeks would have lost weight; no doubt the baby would have been rubbing her throat so much that the skin was reddened raw. Alice would have desperately turned the baby over her knee and patted her on the back in an attempt to dislodge the obstruction, but it was futile. An operation to remove the coin would have been her only salvation, but this type of procedure was only carried out successfully in 1910, too late to save poor little Ethel.

Her second son, also called Robert, was born much later in 1912, and only Maud and Robert survived into adulthood.

Times were hard and infant mortality was high in Victorian Britain; by the latter part of the century, infants under one year old accounted for a quarter of the total deaths in England and Wales. Half of all of the deaths were infants under five. Sanitation and hygiene were serious problems and filth or contaminated foods often caused infection. Diarrhoea was so common and dangerous that it could cause death in a baby in less than 48 hours. The most common life-threatening diseases among older children were scarlet fever, measles, diphtheria and small-pox.

Few remedies existed for sick children of the working class. Because of the expense associated with doctors' services, parents usually considered them only as a last resort. Most parents stuck to home remedies and herbal type potions.

The quality of Victorian home life was poor – tenement buildings were built quickly, and large houses were turned into flats. The cost of rent was extremely high; conditions were often cramped as many members of a single family would live in one room. Many landlords were indifferent to the appalling conditions their tenants were living in and with housing so difficult to find, few made a fuss. Running water, sanitation facilities and even cooking arrangements were rough-shod at best. With tenements consisting of many floors, Victorian Londoners lived cheek-by-jowl with their neighbours. Disputes were commonplace, and often caused by drunkenness.

On the street, petty crimes, such as pick-pocketing and food-snatching, were a regular occurrence. Only a few years before Alice started 'working the stones', Jack the Ripper was stalking Whitechapel by night. The streets of London were often described as 'foggy', caused by the smoke from coal fires and steam paddle boats plying the Thames. Every surface, even the pavements, were covered with a dusting of soot, and you could smell the coal dust in the air. New buildings constructed of Portland stone didn't stay pristine for long – with a combination of raw sewage on the Thames, coal fires, and unwashed bodies, the odour of London was described as being 'memorable' and unhealthy to say the least.

> A lady "scriever," or pavement artist, practises in a West-end thoroughfare. She worked previously in the country, and landscapes seem to be a favourite subject. She is smartly dressed, and appears to be making money.

PRESS CUTTING: Daily Gazette for Middlesbrough;
Wednesday 23 September 1896

Soon after Maud's birth, Alice was back on the streets.

While most newspapers and magazines in 1896 were struck by the sheer novelty of such a sight, some were more interested in Alice's appearance and sense of dress style. The Yorkshire Evening Post described Alice as having "a bored air of weary indifference; and in general effect, resembles Mrs. Patrick Campbell in The Notorious Mrs Ebbsmith."

English stage actress Mrs. Patrick Campbell (Beatrice Stella Tanner)

It's worth noting that most newspaper reports were written by men.

Mrs Patrick Campbell (original name Beatrice Stella Tanner) was an English stage actress born in Kensington – also known as Mrs Pat. *The Notorious Mrs Ebbsmith* was a play by Sir Arthur Wing Pinero. It was first produced on 13 March 1895, with Mrs Patrick Campbell playing the lead role of Agnes Ebbsmith. The theme of the play was social radicalism – the title character is a vehement critic of all social conventions, especially marriage, and an advocate of free love. The lead character Agnes could be described as a revolutionary, an idealist, and full of ideas on new ways that life should be lived. At its premiere in 1895, theatre critic George Bernard Shaw reported "the play is bad," – it has since been described as "a flawed but intriguing curiosity."

Intriguingly, the newspaper reporter aligned Alice with a subversive rebel, and that's exactly what she was, in more ways than one. It may not have been Alice's intention, but the British press liked to play-up this idea of Alice as a defiant anarchist. It's often been speculated that she could have been a member of the women's suffrage movement, but I can find no direct evidence of this. Unlike the Suffragette Chalkers, who appeared ten years later, Alice's work could be described as anything other than political or revolutionary – in fact, it was quite the opposite. In 1896 she was specialising in landscape drawings on the street, as reported by the Coventry Evening Telegraph: "Her snowstorms are quite severe, her sunsets quite as lurid, and her storms-at-sea quite as suggestive as are the similar efforts of any male al fresco artist. Above her pictorial specimens the lady writes: TRULY MY OWN WORK – No Imposture."

Landscapes were, artistically speaking, considered 'conservative'. The stock-in-trade of any self-respecting 19th century pavement artist, they were very popular with the public and brought in the pennies. In her early days Alice tried to be topical, like a newspaper of current events, drawing the most exciting news of the day, such as a murderer's face, or a shipwreck at sea. As a woman 'working the stones' – the technical term for the pavement – she got far more interest and sympathy than the men who considered her to be 'a proper artist with brushes and all'.

Alice received no less than ten proposals of marriage out on the pavements – the possibility of her already being married did not apparently occur to her admirers. The first proposal was made by a Russian 'millionaire.' A notice about her occupation had appeared in one of the Sunday papers, and the would-be wooer sent a letter to her through its editor. The letter was written in Russian.

In 1897, Alice took up a new pitch in the heart of London, opposite the National Gallery, Trafalgar Square. The pitch was outside the Church of St. Martin's-in-the-Field, at the side and opposite the Lowther Arcade (the Golden Cross House today), a popular place for screevers for generations. Places here were much sought after and sometimes even fought over. It was a lucrative spot, where on a good day a pavement artist could earn a lot of money from the passing trade of French, German and English tourists. The fact that she acquired this spot must have meant a certain amount of acceptance on behalf of her male counterparts.

The Graphic Magazine painted this picture of Alice:

"THE Superior Sex is rapidly invading every profession and trade, and in a few years' time miserable man will not have a calling or an avocation that he can call exclusively his own. Let me call your attention to the latest innovation – it is the Lady Screever.

"The other day I saw this clever artist decorating the flags hard by the Church of St. Martin's-in-the-Field on the very spot which was occupied for many years by the well-known blind

20

man and his intelligent dog. As I have known ladies who have gone out in various disguises in London as singers, organ-grinders, and such like, and subsequently given an account of their adventures, I wondered whether this skilful wielder of coloured chalks might be picking up material for a picturesque article.

"She was so daintily costumed, so well-mannered, received the contributions of the passer-by with such an independent grace, that I could scarcely help thinking that she had taken up 'screevery' as an amusement, or for a foundation of experiences, rather than as a profession. The earnestness with which she went down on her knees and dashed in studies and reminiscences of the Upper Thames full of effect and glowing colour bespoke an enthusiasm and an artistic power of someone new to the craft, and there was a feeling for nature and an unconventionality about her pictures that was altogether foreign to everyday screeverism.

"I may be altogether wrong in my suppositions, but still I could not help thinking what a capital article 'The Adventures of a Lady Screever' would make, and what fun the writer might get out of her artistic friends who came and criticised her performances."

Some other members of the journalistic community preferred to focus on Alice's appearance and dress, this feature appeared in the Westminster Budget:

"The female 'screever' has at last arrived in the very heart of London, for she has taken up her 'pitch' under the shadow of St. Martin's Church, usurping for the moment the place hitherto occupied by the gentleman whose pictures hung on the 'line' of the pavement, for he did not draw them every day. The young lady in question is fashionably dressed in a black *alpaca skirt, a light-coloured blouse with a turned-down linen collar, a long tie held in place by a pin, while around her waist is a white

*Petersham belt, fastened with a silverfish buckle, and on her head is a straw hat with a scarlet ribbon.

"Altogether she looks exactly like one of the art students who may be seen winding their way to the National Gallery hard by, the only difference, perhaps, being that her hands bear continual evidence of the manipulation of the chalks which are her tools, an evidence rendering almost supererogatory the inevitable legend that the work is 'all her own, done upon the cold stone,' while she somewhat ostentatiously and affectionately fingers the coppers which have been bestowed upon her by the art-loving passers-by."

*Alpaca was a popular wool material from South America; during Queen Victoria's reign an alpaca coat became an essential item of the wardrobe. It also became part of the family heirloom being passed down through the generation due to its hard wearing ability. A Petersham belt or ribbon was very fashionable and came in many different colours and designs; they are still in use today.

Alice didn't stay in one place, she was moving around London and was seen popping-up all over – as one newspaper put it "A rather pretty young woman has begun business as a pavement artist on London street corners."

Guernsey's Star Newspaper reported: "A woman has successfully asserted her claim to paint for the People's Academy, and in one of the northern suburbs a feminine artist can be seen day after day working deftly in familiar vermilion and yellow ochre."

She was seen in the West End, Grays Inn Road, and many other places where passers-by were appreciative and contributed coppers liberally. While her male counterparts were making anything up to 2 shillings a day (£11 today) Alice was earning in excess of 5 shillings a day, tax free! (£28 today) Of course, rain or even a small shower could scupper a day's work and make it difficult to make anything at all. So the saying *"saving something for a rainy day"* had a real meaning for the English screever. When the fine drizzling rain and murky greyness started stealing up the street, artists melted away like butter on toast.

A LADY PAVEMENT ARTIST.

Alice Colman, as described in the Westminster Budget

....

"Sometimes I felt downhearted when the rain came and washed away a morning's work, but I soon learned that it is no use crying over a spoilt drawing or two. Sometimes, on the other hand, I felt that I would like to take away a flagstone after I had drawn a particularly good one, for I love pretty colours."

....

Many wild and wonderful stories had found their way into print about the 'vast profits' that pavement artists were earning – some journalists decided to test out the theory, by going undercover, disguising themselves as screevers to see if the streets of London really were paved with gold.

Of course, it was a complete myth and although Alice was making a fair amount on a good day, many days she could earn next to nothing. Being a pavement artist was no easy life, and in a day without the welfare system we enjoy today, it was often one of the very few options in keeping yourself and your family out of the 'casual ward' – one drawing away from the workhouse.

....

"Bad days occur all too frequently and wet weather of course means no work at all."

....

The days were often long and unpredictable. During the summer months, Alice would work from between 2pm and 8pm. She would be required to remove her pictures every evening using a duster and water. In general, the police would tolerate screevers as long as they cleaned their pitches, and did not cause an obstruction to pavement traffic.

Each day was like a stage performance and every set of pictures produced was referred to as a "SHOW."

Alice had a particular way of working and a set of daily routines; before starting work she would set out all her chalks and kit on the pavement and make it comfortable. Preparing the pitch and organising herself was an important part of the process – it marked out a professional from an opportunist.

It's true to say that nobody but a pavement artist knows how great the amount of dust is on a London street. Clearing the space is the first job, so a cloth duster came in useful. Alice is known to have used Bath bricks to help create a suitable surface for the chalks. These were made from fine clay and were similar in size to an ordinary house brick; they could be broken up and used in a number of ways. It's most likely that Alice used the bricks to create a smooth and even background for her drawings. She would do this by coating the flagstone with 'cold water size' then, while the surface was wet, rub it down with the Bath brick; this gave a smooth surface, and made the chalks sparkle bright and clear. Some artists used sugared water to help the chalks adhere better to the pavement, and prevent the wind blowing the chalks away.

Alice's kit would have included:

- a little mat to kneel on
- a basket to carry equipment
- home-made chalks (typically made from chalk powder, pigment and condensed milk)
- bath brick, for background preparation
- 3 or 4 candles (for night screeving)
- a duster, for preparation and cleaning the pitch at the end of day
- a tin tray for public contributions (sometimes she used a mother-of-pearl shell)
- an orange box to sit on

It was a generally agreed etiquette that artists should clean their pitch at the end of the day. Doing so avoided hassle with the police and fellow screevers. Another reason for cleaning the pitch was to ensure that nobody came along and claimed the work as being their own, and so started making money from someone else's hard work. It would also 'crool the pitch', were members of the public would feel deceived if they gave money to a man one day only to find a completely different man doing the same pictures in the same spot the next day.

....

"I chalk ten pictures for each pitch"

....

Most of Alice's work would have been done from memory – accumulated knowledge gained from repeating similar scenes and designs again and again. To the casual bystander, this can appear like a magical gift. Chalks and pastels are an excellent and tactile medium for blending colours. After preparing her surface, Alice would start off by drawing a simple outline in white chalk and then quickly adding areas of colour which would be rubbed down and blended using the palm of the hand. Each finger would be used in a similar way as you would use a different-sized paint brush. Colours would be brought into harmonies and then the finishing touches were made using pointed pieces of coloured chalk. With practice, a simple landscape could be done in ten minutes. The art was kept small, usually taking up one flagstone each. Artists had to establish their works in the shortest possible time to attract the attention of the passers-by.

....

"I find a salmon or mackerel, very brightly coloured, of most interest to the public. They never grow tired of looking at these. Then the rustic bridge scene goes down very well, and groups of flowers and fruit are always popular. To appeal to the street public one has always to draw gay pictures. The skies have to be very blue and the trees of the greenest green."

....

PAVEMENT ARTISTS.

Inquiry was made at the London County Council on Tuesday regarding pavement artists on the Thames embankment, who need no license or permit. It was stated that the police do not interfere unless there is obstruction.

PRESS CUTTING: Gloucester Citizen

The work was set hard against a wall or railings to avoid causing an obstruction; artists could be moved on or even arrested if the pavements became obstructed. Alice had a lunch break every day and often a fellow screever would mind her pitch while she was away. She sometimes sat by the River Thames with a packed lunch and often attracted a little cloud of cockney sparrows, looking for scraps. They would nest in abundance under the newly installed arc-lamps along the Embankment and were generally loved by the kindly screever who would toss bits of bread. Londoners have always had a special connection with 'Thou brave and faithful Sparrow'.

The public's perception of pavement artists was fickle and changed with the wind. Fine and sunny days were perfect, and people were more generous at parting with their 'browns'. Very hot days made them hot and bothered and trade would be sluggish. On cold and grey days, passers-by could be grumpy and over critical. Just by looking out of the window, artists got to know instinctively what type of day it was going to be. On the whole, people enjoyed seeing the pavement artists, especially if they displayed real artistry.

Artists had a few tricks to illicit extra coins; engaging a passer-by in conversation could work wonders in loosening the purse strings, as could greeting regulars with a pleasant smile and a cheerful greeting. Strategically placing a hat or dish at both ends of the pitch helped, and catching the eye of anybody who gave even the most fleeting of interests in the art; works that appealed to children would do wonders for creating 'pester power.' And not forgetting to acknowledge everybody who tossed in a 'brown' with a cheery 'thank-you' and 'good luck to you!'

A day on the flags was no easy option; sore knees, aching back and cramps in the legs were all part of the course, not to mention raw and sometimes bleeding fingers, depending how rough the surface was. The rub of the surface is everything to pavement artists: too smooth and the chalk would lay on the surface and blow off with the wind; too rough and the chalks would break up and crumble. The stones had to be just right, and the newly-laid York stone along the Embankment was perfect – 'like butter', as one artist described it.

CHAPTER TWO

The Embankment

The streets are strange levellers; they form a common ground upon which all ranks meet on equal terms – where no one – no matter how lofty or distinguished – has more rights or advantages than the most humble members of society.

Victoria Embankment begins after Westminster Bridge and is lined with plane trees, softening the towering architecture that lines its route. During the day it was a popular place to promenade, and at night, the lamplight among the leaves made the trip by the water particularly attractive.

The Yorkshire Evening Post reported: "Members of Parliament passing along the Thames Embankment lately have seen, not without interest, that absolutely the only female pavement artist in London has taken a place not far from Big Ben."

The year was 1899, and after a brief appearance in the 'northern suburbs' (Leighton Buzzard), Alice took up her new pitch on the Victoria Embankment; she favoured a spot near the corner, not far from Westminster Bridge and directly opposite the Houses of Parliament. She had been working as a pavement artist for five years, and at the tender age of 25, was still considered as 'youngish' by the popular press.

In an interview with the Leeds Times, Alice explained: "I can make a picture in 10 minutes. You see I have got five here. I chiefly go in for landscapes. There is a bridge there – an English bridge. It usually has a horse going over the top, but it is so warm today that he has taken refuge in the stream beneath. I repaint my pictures every day, but they are usually on the same subjects. I find a subject that takes with the public, and stick to it. But those mackerel may become salmon tomorrow."

That independent feeling of being a professional woman, pursuing her own creative work and being paid must have been empowering for Alice, and more importantly, kept the pot boiling at home.

Screevers were a common sight on the streets of Victorian London. The Daily Mirror's 'Wonderful London' feature in 1913 surveyed 'children from the country', asking them what would be in their top ten on visiting London? No surprises to hear that *"Seeing those FUNNY MEN drawing on the pavements!"* came top of the list.

George Orwell's *Down and Out in Paris and London* repeated the oft-quoted fact of the time – that a pavement artist could be found every 25 feet along the Thames Embankment. As still happens today, tourists and locals would enjoy a pleasant amble along the river; during morning and evening rush hours, artists would pick up a brisk trade from passing commuters. It was as bustling then as now: to the screever's dismay, a little old lady would come daily to feed the seagulls on the Embankment. Hundreds of birds would flock down; unable to compete, the artists retreated to a safe distance until the melee had passed. If the artist and their work escaped attack by the birds, they still had perambulators and unwieldy children running over the art – not to mention the over-excited dogs with muddy paws!

The Embankment was full of all kinds of people trying to make ends meet, like the old man at the corner of Westminster Bridge who, for a penny, would let you peer through his glittering, brass-mounted telescope at the hands of Big Ben, and give you a dog-eared postcard of the great clock with a profound description of its works. The muffin man, with his dulcet cries of 'Hawt muffeens, muffeens, hawt muffeens!' and the sweet floating strains of the Italian organ grinder and his monkey, dancing dogs, the match vendor and the singing Irish Girls, as children's nannies gossiped under the shade of the plane trees. A blind beggar in a tall hat stood at the edge of the kerbstone holding a tray of matches and boot laces to sell; his stick in one hand nervously tapped the inch of pavement by his side.

Red caps and black sun bonnets could be seen in the distance on Sundays as the Salvation Army held its meetings by the river, with flags flying and loud brass instruments playing serenades to the slow moving river traffic.

The Embankment was full of characters; you were lucky if you saw little 'Tinkle-Tink' – he usually worked around Leicester Square but would occasionally head to the river for a breath of fresh air. He was the street entertainer who got his name from the faint, piping tunes that came mysteriously from some invisible instrument hidden in the folds of an immense brown cloak. He was said to have entertained everybody who ever had any business to walk through Coventry Street.

Then there was old bearded 'Omar', who – between snoozes in the museum library and frequent adjournments to the local pub – would recite Virgil and the *Rubalyat of Omar Khayyam* for sixpence. Omar would also be keen to talk street philosophy to anybody who would care to listen – as the crowd gathered, he would proclaim, booming at the top of his voice, 'One by one the lowliest and the best vanish into the mazes of this mighty city'.

'Little Nell', a West End flower girl, worked around the Embankment and Leicester Square for over 40 years. She was a London landmark, wrapped in brown paper like a store parcel on wintry days. On very cold days, she had the unfortunate habit of covering her arms and legs in dripping or goose fat. She would be seen walking to her pitch, balancing a large wicker basket full of flowers on her head.

But on a good day, nothing could compete with watching the row of pavement pastellists, stretching as far as the eye could see, creating their colourful outdoor galleries.

THE LADY PAVEMENT ARTIST.

Alice Colman on Victoria Embankment: Lloyds Weekly Newspaper –
Sunday 30 July 1899

There were portraits – and clever cartoons – of famous politicians: Mr Gladstone; Mr Balfour and Lord Salisbury – and if you didn't happen to recognise them, their names were written underneath in perfect copperplate. There were vivid landscapes with names like '*Eventide*', chalked with an elaborate confection of distant, sheep dotted fields; a blue river that rippled like a snake round the foot of a spired church, and a shepherd with dog and crook; the whole picture lit by the glow of a lurid sunset... A portrait of 'Her Majesty the Queen, God Bless Her' would sit next door to a figure-of-eight loaf and a piece of ruddily-blushing salmon, each on a plate white as snow. The caption 'Easy to Draw, Hard to Get' and a coin dropped into a ringing tin cup was greeted with a 'Thankee, kind sir' by the pavement artist with a certain glow of appreciation.

A little further down, on the rise of Westminster Bridge, was a newcomer to the ancient fraternity of flagstone artists: a boy who obviously couldn't draw took up a pitch and tried his best at depicting a pear, a plum, an orange and a pink heart. But it was hard to draw on the stones, and his chalks were few and poor. Underneath his drawings were the inscription "I am the eldest of six brothers and sisters, and our father has died and left us totally unprovided for, and this is all I can do to help as yet, for I am only ten years old."

A few pitches down from Alice worked 'Pigeon Boy'. So-called because his sketching powers were limited to the depiction of pigeons, legend has it he did them so well you would almost think they were real. And on a good day 'Lonely Jack' would put in an appearance on the pavement stage; he could draw a fillet of salmon better than any man alive. Reckoned to be the best screever in London, he always drew a good crowd.

Pavement artists came in all shapes and sizes, classes and religions; poverty had no respect for such superficial ideals, and there go anybody but for the grace of circumstance. When

Alice started in 1893, successful and eminent Pre-Raphaelite painter Simeon Solomon had begun to hit the bottle, and taken up a pitch on the Embankment, but he was later moved on to Bayswater. The artist and designer Edward Burne-Jones described him as being 'the greatest artist of us all,' but he drifted into 'bad ways' and all the efforts of his friends failed to save him. He had a pitch on Brompton Road, but didn't make enough money to support himself, so took to hawking matches. He was found one night in August 1895, drunk and unconscious in the street at Holborn; he was taken to the nearest infirmary, and there a week later he died.

Every artist and street peddler had a story to tell.

The average screever was described as being male and 'greasy'; not over-clean in language and sometimes smelling of drink. They were nicknamed 'the shabby pastellists' or 'the gutter cartoonists' by some, on account of their unshaven and dilapidated, come-down-in-the-world look. Alice was – according to the Edinburgh Evening News – in total contrast "well dressed, fashionable, well-educated and refined." The Leeds Times went as far to say that the Thames Embankment had been 'enriched' by her presence.

A reader of the Westminster Gazette sent in a letter giving an eloquent description of Alice at her pitch; "Early one beautiful spring morning, when even the London air smelt fresh and pure, we looked out from our corner house and saw a pavement artist at work. To our surprise it was a girl. A young and really pretty girl, quite charmingly dressed, in a little flowered cotton blouse, neatly belted to the waist and the daintiest of straw hats. She carried with her a small box of colours, and carefully taking off her gloves she laid them on this when she had taken out her materials for work. When all was done, she looked hastily round, drew on her gloves again and marched away.

Alice on the Thames Embankment: Leeds Times – Saturday 5 August 1899

"She came every morning, and every morning we were at the window to watch and wonder. It struck us in a flash that this was no ordinary pavement artist."

In an interview with the Advertiser in Adelaide, Alice revealed: "I have made many friends on the street, people who kindly look out for me. One gentleman got me an engagement at a school, to draw simple things for the children."

Every day, hundreds, if not thousands, of people would pass Alice working on the Embankment. From the men, women and children who passed every day, she was building up a following of regular patrons and art lovers. Some would commission her to do portraits and particular landscapes, while others would simply show their appreciation by dropping a couple of coins in her tray on a daily basis; every passer-by was a potential 'patron of the arts.'

Alice had had drawing lessons, but continued to develop her craft as she worked at her screeving: "I have had lessons in drawing, but the colouring is entirely after my own ideas," she told Sydney's The World's News.

The Victorians were great lovers of the picturesque, and often admiring crowds would gather around particularly good artists; they preferred nature and landscapes, but also liked sentiment and pathos. Pictures of bright colours and hues were the most popular; there was a trend of what became known as 'degenerate artists' who, instead of painstakingly daubing the same pitch day after day, brought out a series of highly-coloured oil pictures on cardboard, that were often hired out from other artists, and were obviously NOT their own work; these types were hated by the true pavement artist, and the public quickly discovered them to be nothing more than opportunistic and hollow frauds. The most successful artist was the one who cleaned off their pitch every night, and started a fresh batch of drawings on-the-spot every day.

Alice did take issue against the boardmen – the artists who exhibited chalk studies of shipwrecks and salmon on boards. 'Absolute frauds,' she would call them. According to Alice, the boards were hired by the day, like costers' barrows, and returned at night to the 'firms' who deal in them. But she did agree that there were a good number of male artists, who 'although limited in their scope,' were genuine enough.

In the same World's News feature, the journalist described Alice's work: "Mrs Colman had drawn a panorama of landscapes interspersed with two beautiful green parrots, a tempting-looking mackerel, and a pretty spray of pink carnations. Her landscapes comprised of a lake with a towering mountain on the right, behind which the setting sun was casting a golden shimmer on the water. On another lake, two white swans were sunning themselves. They could not be swimming, for there was not a ripple on the water, which, like a sheet of glass, reflected the trees on the banks.

"A third sketch represented a windmill at the edge of a dusty road, and a fourth depicted a castle. Chalked notices proclaimed the production 'Truly my own work, drawn without a copy,' and Mrs Colman gave proof of this by adding to her 'gallery' with rapidity. One of the parrots was represented as saying Live and let live."

In general, most screevers were considered gifted, and often with a fair amount of technical ability. The feeling was that, given happier circumstances and less acquaintance with the bar of the local public house, these artists' efforts could well be exhibited on the hallowed walls of the Royal Academy.

★★★★★

Alice's third child Ethel Mary Colman was born in March 1900, and the lady screever was making a decent living. Her husband Robert was on the mend and well enough to join Alice on the streets. He had been a pavement artist long before they met. Their day would start early – after breakfast, and leaving the children with the grand parents, they would leave the house and go their separate ways. Robert was still partially paralysed and walked with a pronounced limp. The couple rarely worked together on the same pitch, but rather hedged their bets by working in two different locations, hoping that if one area was slow going, the other would prove more profitable.

Robert's disability also worked in his favour – the public loved a hard luck story. Some artists would use a dog to gain sympathy and extra pennies while others were helped by babies, hired out for the day from street gangs.

Pavement artists were open to all kinds of threats and dangers

The screever treasured their little bit of pavement. The flagstones the serious artists used for their canvas required months of preparation and smoothing to make the pitch just right. Gangs watched this work with great interest – once the artist had settled down, he was told he needed protection.

If he didn't agree to pay, his life would become unbearable. It would start with minor irritations… a broken bottle of oil, accidentally spilled by a careless passer-by, just after the morning's work was finished made a re-drawing necessary. Before long, the pavement artist conceded defeat and opted for protection. It saved him from being beaten up and robbed on the way home, or his pitch being covered in petrol and tar. Artists were often forced to buy their chalks from the gang boss, at extortionate prices.

Pitches worked by the boardmen and their movable pictures were milked differently. Artists had to rent the pitch by the hour; the pictures were rented from criminal gangs. Artists hired babies and dogs from the gang to help them; a pathetic-looking dog would cost more to hire than a good-looking dog. Artists without fixed pitches benefitted less from regular customers, but were the most difficult to exploit, so racketeers would send out inspectors', who travelled across London, working on commission and extorting money from the casual screever or beggar.

All this was a pretty small scale operation in 1900 and there is no evidence that either Alice or Robert were the victims of street bullies, but they did exist, and the more money that street artists earned, the more of a target they became.

A more frequent hazard were the daily abuses from the drunken art critic or workman tipsily staggering home after one too many. "Blest if I couldn't dror better meself" he would mutter, exhibiting an inclination to fall down and go to sleep on the despised pictures. Then there was the daily battle of the sexes with fellow pavement artists, all of whom were men, and resented a woman infringing on 'man's work'. This was published in the Sheffield Telegraph in 1901:

"The rivalry of the sexes may be sustained on various grounds. Two screevers were watching a lady pavement artist in Kensington yesterday, with disapproval largely written all over their faces. *'They leave us nothing – not even the pavement to make an honest livin' out of!'* looking with unwilling admiration at her portrait of the King in reds and yellows."

This resentment was partly fuelled by the growing women's suffrage movement. By 1907 the Suffragette movement had discovered the power of street art to support and further its political aims. Difficult to control and outside the social 'establishment', temporary pavement art became a key tactic to announce meetings, raise funds and gain popular support for the Woman's Suffrage movement. Female artists would take over pitches pronouncing 'Votes for Woman' and 'Spare a Penny for the WSPU' (Woman's Social and Political Union).

But there were also the unforeseen dangers of spending all day on your hands and knees on the pavement. In May 1900, Alice had a narrow escape; she was kneeling down, hard at work with her chalks, outside the churchyard railings on Pentonville Hill, when the horses pulling a brewer's dray got out of control and bolted. Intent upon her work, Alice was quite oblivious to the commotion about her, until the dray crashed onto the pavement. She looked up to find the hooves of the foremost horse practically on her head. With the animal's hot breath in her face, she sprang into the gateway of the churchyard – an instant later, horses and dray were heaped up, a confused mass upon her drawings. Only a few years later, in almost the same spot, a pavement artist was crushed to death by a new-fangled horseless carriage (motor-car).

CHAPTER THREE

A Woman's Progress

Queen Victoria died on 22 January 1901, and on 2 February, the day of the Queen's state funeral, the weather was described as cloudy, fairly cold, but dry. Pavement artists were out in force, monopolising the huge crowds that had descended upon the capital. Portraits of the late Queen – 'God Bless Her Soul' – were the order of the day. Big events were big business for the humble screever. Britain had entered the Edwardian era, a period of great change and uncertainty. Victoria's eldest son, Edward VII was now on the throne, and London was still the largest and most important city in the world.

Times were changing. By the turn of the century, stern Victorian values had given way to a more liberal Edwardian society – change was afoot; women were becoming organised, demanding the vote and pavement artists became a pictorial poor man's newspaper of world events; part escapism, part social commentary.

It would be wrong to view pavement artists exclusively as victims of circumstance – a poor man's artist eking out a living on the margins of society. It's true that some did fall into this category, but it was also a lifestyle choice – the chance to be admired daily by thousands of passers-by and to be remunerated to create art in a public place. Screevers were regarded as beggars by the authorities, but this was only part of the truth. While some chancers did beg and pray upon people's charitable natures, a lot of the true artists, the good ones, entered into an unspoken 'trade' between screever and viewer: 'if you like my work and you can spare a copper then please do so'... Rarely did a screever hold out his hand asking people for money. As with any other form of busking, this was a fair exchange; I've beautified the pavements for your enjoyment and if you appreciate it then gratuities would be welcome. The deal was mutually understood, but there would always be chancers and scam merchants looking to cash in on a successful artist's pitch.

In 1906, E. V. Lucas gave this wonderful account in his guide book, *A Wanderer in London*. It describes a screeving pitch around St. Martin's in the Field, just off Trafalgar Square: "The pavements to the north & south used to be the canvas of two very superior 'screevers' – as men are called who make pastel drawings on paving stones. London has fewer 'screevers' than it used, and latterly I have noticed among such of these artists as remain a growing tendency to bring oil paintings (which may or may not be their own work) and lean them against the wall, supplying themselves only the minimum of scroll work beneath. To such go no pennies of mine – unless of course the day is dripping wet. On dry pavement the 'screever' must show us his pictures in the making: they must like hot rolls, be new every morning. We will have no scamping in this art.'

The First World War was fast approaching and the political landscape of Britain would never be the same again. The high water-mark of British political screeving was over; more important things were afoot.

Living London

Alice was 27, and the Colman family lived at 8, Bransford Street, Kensington. They were so proud of their profession that Robert even declared himself a pavement artist in the 1901 census. At that time, the woman's occupation was not declared.

Alice was featured in the part-work book *Living London*, edited by George R. Sims and published by Cassell. It was sold in weekly parts that built to a complete first volume, containing

1901 Census: Alice and Robert Colman.
Robert registered his profession as 'pavement artist'

A LADY PAVEMENT ARTIST.—*From "Living London."* *Edited by G. R. Sims, and published Fortnightly, 7d. net, by Cassell and Co., Limited.*

Dear Nurse the train was an hour late. has all the snow gone yet. Hubert likes me very much and gets his games and lets me play with lots of love Leila

Dec 15th 1901

Alice postcard, published by Cassell: 1901

over 450 illustrations and photographs, with 404 pages. Collectors could buy each weekly part, then complete the volume with a binder to put the editions in. Cassell was the first to pioneer this very popular kind of publishing – *Living London* was designed to show the world's greatest city at work and play; its humour, its pathos, its sights, and its scenes.

To promote the book, they published a series of postcards, one of which featured Alice – the Lady Pavement Artist. *Living London* was a prestigious publication, and Alice's unique story was a key part of its marketing.

This Press Cutting from the Sunderland Daily Echo and Shipping Gazette (Friday 3 October, 1902), describes *'The Latest Encroachment':*

"Still more encroachments upon the masculine preserve, writes a correspondent. Hitherto the profession of the pavement artist has been the exclusive prerogative of the indigent male who has supplemented the appeals of art by the more eloquent pleas of a wooden leg or an exaggerated squint.

"But we have changed all that at Hampstead. Coming down the high-street yesterday I beheld a lady neatly and prettily attired bending over the pavement, on which she had drawn a series of excellent scenes.

"The pavement artists, new style, struck me as a distinct improvement on the old style, and it suggests a new sphere of labour for – must we use the discourteous phrase? – superfluous woman."

It was 1906 when Alice took up a new pitch on Kingsway, a brand new road, purpose-built as part of a major redevelopment of the area. Its route cleared away the maze of small streets in Holborn such as Little Queen Street and the surrounding slum dwellings, and was considered so grand that even trams were forced to go underground when the first ever tram tunnel was built underneath the road. This new redeveloped area of

LADY PAVEMENT-ARTIST IN THE KINGSWAY.

The efforts of a lady pavement-artist in the Kingsway yesterday attracted many admirers, and she reaped a rich harvest. The photograph on the left shows the artist at work. On the right she is seen standing by her packet of chalks.—(*Daily Mirror* photographs.)

PRESS CUTTING: Daily Mirror; Thursday 15 November 1906.
Alice, the lady pavement artist

London offered pavement artists new opportunities as it quickly became popular with business types and people with disposable incomes.

In its column *A Woman's Progress*, the *Evening Telegraph* reported:

"The lady pavement artist is the newest modern product. This pioneer of the sex in an occupation hitherto purely masculine has taken up her stand appropriately enough, in London's newest thoroughfare, Kingsway; to be more exact, on the right-hand side leaving Holborn in the direction of the Strand.

"Other lady artists have from time to time made fitful appearances in the outlying districts, but this one has come right into the Metropolis, and says she has come to stay.

A FAIR "SCREEVER" AT WORK IN KINGSWAY: LONDON'S LADY PAVEMENT-ARTIST
AT HER PITCH.

London's fair pavement-artist has taken up her stand in Kingsway, on the right-hand side of the road coming towards the Strand. Her working hours are from 2 p.m. until 8 p.m.

Photograph by the Illustrations Bureau.

Alice Colman at her pitch in Kingsway, London aged 32
(published in The Sketch, 1906)

"She is a comely, self-possessed young woman, whose working hours are from 2pm till 8pm. Her ideas as to art include all that any pavement artist can teach her, and it is a pleasure to see how the vivid-coloured mackerel and the familiar windmill which have delighted so many pedestrians spring up before her nimble touch.

"The lady artist dresses very neatly in a light blouse and a black skirt, and in order not to soil her attire uses a mat. Whilst awaiting the shower of coppers she sits on an orange box."

As a woman, Alice's choices in life were very limited, and most young working class women went into domestic service. Long hours and poor pay was the order of the day. In spite of the challenges she faced, Alice enjoyed the freedom and recognition of her job. In a 1903 interview with Adelaide's *The Advertiser,* she told the journalist: "I do not think of changing my profession, except, perhaps, for the lightening cartoon business. I tried my hand at that once, at a seaside music hall, where I had got an engagement, and although I was simply trembling with nervousness I did fairly well, to judge by the kindness and applause of the audience."

Naturally she was very proud of her work, and was not slow to assess the work of those amateurs who, instead of decorating the pavements, brought with them pictures finished at home. 'All my own work' was the bold legend surmounting each of her artistic achievements. 'There is no fraud about my pictures. They are done on the spot.'

> A smartly dressed lady has now established her pitch as pavement artist at the Holborn end of Kingsway.

Manchester Courier and Lancashire General Advertiser –
Wednesday 22 August, 1906

Although there is no evidence that Alice was a formal member of the Women's Suffrage movement, it is likely that she did have sympathies for the movement – even at the time, some newspapers took her for being a suffragette. The *London Chronicle* reported on the "Suffragette Pavement Artist; a smartly dressed lady has now established her pitch as pavement artist at the Holborn end of Kingsway."

By 1902, the National Union of Women's Suffrage Societies (the Suffragettes) were gaining political momentum for their campaign for equal rights and VOTES FOR WOMEN. Formed in 1897 from a collection of local suffrage societies (five years after Alice first made her mark on the streets of London) the

Suffragettes were becoming increasingly high profile, and gaining attention from the press.

Alice's appearance on the streets did nothing to harm the Women's Suffrage movement, and quite possibly inspired their own pavement chalking campaigns. Members of the suffrage movement were mostly, but not exclusively, women from middle class backgrounds, frustrated by their social and economic situation and seeking an outlet through which to initiate change. Alice was acutely aware of her position as an outsider, telling *Adelaide's Advertiser:* "unfortunately, since I took to this sort of calling, I have met with much opposition from men engaged in the same pursuit. I have not set myself up against them. If it was not a matter of necessity, I should not be here at all."

Pavement Art as a tactic for social change

Between 1906 and 1914, the Suffragettes organised a sustained chalking campaign for social change and political rights for women. They would organise 'chalking parties.' 'Lady chalkers', as the newspapers called them, had to be careful and were advised to go in twos or threes, never alone: purple, white and green chalk was used. The tricolore symbolised dignity (purple), purity (white) and hope (green) – these three colours were used for banners, flags, rosettes and badges, and appeared in newspaper cartoons and postcards; the colour scheme was formally adopted by the WSPU in 1908.

Pavement chalking was used to announce meetings, demonstrations and express protest. In 1908, Emma Sproson (suffragette, socialist and Wolverhampton's first female councillor, she was also known as Red Emma) became the first suffragette to be summoned by the courts for chalking on the pavement. She was fined five shillings, and endured two periods of imprisonment for her suffragette militancy.

Although these anarchic chalkings on the pavement could not be considered 'art' in its truest sense, it did open the

'This is the house that man built': Suffragette postcard c.1910

floodgates for fellow suffragettes to claim pavement art as a vehicle for political and social change. It was the subversive nature of chalking on the flagstones and the potential martyrdom of arrest that appealed to the militant artists. The message of the Women's Social and Political Union, which had been gagged and twisted by the popular press, could now freely be expressed 'word of mouth' on the streets.

Female pavement artists would screeve messages imploring passers-by: 'Votes for Women-Self Denial Week-Spare a Penny!' Artists would take along examples of original artwork for sale to public sympathisers and this fast became an important fundraising exercise by the WSPU.

Suffragette Marie Brackenbury studied at the prestigious Slade School of Art in London and became a talented landscape painter, but became a pavement artist for the women's suffrage cause. In 1908 she designed a postcard showing a series of nine drawings with captions, giving the suffragette view of Parliament. 'History up to date and more so by a Suffragette Pavement Artist' – these 'fund-raising' postcards were sold on the street during Self-Denial Week and at political meetings throughout the year.

In order to raise funds, campaigner and WSPU president Emmeline Pethick-Lawrence designated 15 to 22 February 1908 as Self-Denial week. WSPU members went without luxuries including cocoa, coffee and tea, performed extra work, or used other means – such as pavement chalking – to raise funds for the Union. Talking about Self-Denial Week, Pethick-Lawrence revealed that "some of the members who were artists meant to add to the funds by working as pavement artists, while other intended to sing in the streets." Christabel Pankhurst later reported, "the results from street singing, organ playing, and pavement drawing have been excellent!" 1908's Self-Denial Week raised over £8,000 for the suffrage movement – £672,851 in today's value.

THE LADY PAVEMENT ARTIST.

The advent of the lady shoeblack has been followed by the lady pavement artist. A young lady has taken up her position in Kingsway, where she reaps a goodly income with her artistic pavement pictures.

PRESS CUTTING: Daily Express, Thursday 23 August 1906

Postcard in the Suffragette colours of green, white and purple, c.1907

Suffragette pavement artists 1913

Suffragette pavement artists 1913

It was apparent that these middle class do-gooders were gaining popular support outside the establishment. Individuals showed their support by publishing postcards for sale featuring 'Lady Pavement Artists' – well dressed women of refinement were photographed on their hands and knees, producing art on the street. Yet incredibly, it wasn't all political – they would produce works simply to entertain and enthral the public with technique and artistry.

Political pavement chalking was not a new invention; cartoons and side-swipes at the politicians of the day was something that had been practiced on the streets of England for well over 100 years. It was from the very same tradition that gave birth to Punch Magazine.

Set up by social reformer Henry Mayhew on 17 July 1841, the first edition of Punch – or the London Charivari Magazine – was published and the political and satirical cartooning of the streets was taken into the realms of the printed page. In the 1840s, Mayhew had observed, documented and described the London screever in his seminal work *London Labour and the London Poor*. In his book, pavement artists were classed as 'Street Artisans', in many respects a cut above your average beggar. It's no surprise that Punch featured pavement artists to make political points as an effective weapon to the political satirist. Punch often published cartoons of pavement artists as a form of political metaphor.

More recently, Bristol graffiti artist Banksy has made a career out of lampooning social values and institutions like the police and the armed forces. This kind of 'guerrilla' warfare fodder between the street artist and the powers-that-be is nothing new – pavement artists have been doing it for a long time, and it would be a misconception to believe that all screevers just drew 'pretty pictures' on the pavements for public entertainment and gratuities. The most successful artists attracted the crowds (and the money) by creating pictorial lampoons on contemporary

Glass lantern slide: an artist working along the Thames Embankment c.1900

events. This tradition of mocking the establishment had been documented since at least the early 1800s and long before television or the internet were ever dreamed of, the political pavement artist was king.

They often attracted large crowds of 'street-passengers' and would have look-outs, keeping an eye out for the *peelers* (policemen). Big cities like London, Birmingham, Manchester and Liverpool attracted the largest crowds and the skilled screever could find their pockets bulging with pennies at the end of a successful day's work.

Large crowds gathered quickly from small causes, and pavement artists would try to find an out-of-the-way spot, where the peelers would take time to find and disperse them. They had to work fast – often the works were small in scale so that the message and theme was established quickly to attract passing trade. It was important to draw with rapidity; not with the rapidity of slovenliness, but with the rapidity of a genius in the choice of what became known as 'fateful lines.'

Screevers attracted large crowds – glass lantern slide of George Blaber
at his pitch in Nottingham c.1906

Screevers played to the gallery of the common man and woman and would often mix satirical drawings of politicians, peelers and public figures with the prize fighters of the day. Crowds would cheer at the sight of a topical boxing match and laugh at the buffoonery of a comically drawn peeler. A politician involved in scandal and debauchery was fair game to the masses. A picture spoke a thousand words and, in a world where poor people were largely unable to read and write, the pavement artist was perfectly placed to convey a message to ordinary folk. Working outside the establishment, and yet clever enough to be a self-taught drawer, they were frowned upon by the well-to-do, who saw them as little more than beggars.

The screever paid a heavy price if caught; the peeler, often vindictive, would march them off, away from the crowds, and give them a severe beating down a side street before carting them off to the gaol. It was a continual battle between police and screevers, who were classed as being little better than beggars, thieves and pickpockets and often imprisoned and under the new 1834 Poor Law – they were sent to workhouses designed to 'rid the streets of beggars and vagrants' and 'prevent scroungers' and 'screevers' from littering the streets.

Liverpool pavement artist James Carling offered a nice insight to the world of the Victorian screever – he described his brothers, Willy, Johnny and Henry as 'rollicking street artists', who became 'political lampooners of the municipal government'. If the screever had no look-out they would ask the crowds at intervals 'is the peeler coming?' and pick a place with lots of side streets to disappear down. James Carling recalled Christmas Eve 1865, when he had been out all day drawing on the city's Elliot Street to make some Christmas money. Towards the end of the day he moved to Lime Street and posted a chum as a look-out for the peelers, and began drawing a comical caricature of a policeman, when he was jerked to his feet by a peeler, beaten and hustled off to Cheapside jail, where he spent Christmas Eve before being ordered to spend six years in St. George's Industrial School. He was just eight years of age. Political street cartoonists were barely tolerated by the Victorian authorities, but they spoke to the ordinary folk who rewarded them with coppers for their efforts.

Boy pavement artist James Carling in Liverpool, c.1869

CHAPTER FOUR

The Music Hall

"Underneath the railway arch, not really far away
I knows a pavement artist who draws pictures every day
With little bits of coloured chalk he draws his ideas out
They look so real you fancy you can see em move about."

The Pavement Artist, music hall song by Gus Elen, 1906

Alice came from a theatrical background, and she and her husband enjoyed the Music Hall; whenever they could afford it, they would spend evenings in the West End watching their favourite stars and participating in audience singsongs.

Music halls were very much working class entertainment, traced back to the pubs and coffee houses of 18th century London where men met to eat, drink and do business. Performers sang songs whilst the audience ate, drank and joined in the singing. By the 1830s pubs had rooms devoted to musical clubs, and these eventually evolved into fully-fledged theatrical performances. Singing, dancing, drama, comedy and novelty acts were all part of an evening's entertainment.

In 1906, music hall singer and comedian, Gus Elen wrote and performed his famous pavement artist routine to packed houses throughout Britain. The US-based Logansport Pharos-Tribune said in 1907 that "There is a vital touch to everything that Mr Elen does, and his comedy is so unctuous that his vogue in London is easily understood. He awoke the house to enthusiasm, which did not diminish with the succeeding efforts, and the audience would gladly have listened to more like his tale of THE PAVEMENT ARTIST."

Alice's greatest thrill was a night out at the Bioscope attraction, a travelling cinema. The first films were shown at music hall in around 1896 and consisted of moving images of city street scenes from around the world. Short comic chase films and romances like *A Soldier's Courtship* all captured the public's imagination. News films were shown at the end of the variety programme. The evenings were packed and proved so popular that proprietors started to open their own purpose-built cinemas. The age of the pictures – the flicks – had arrived.

1907 was the year of the Music Hall Strike, and for two weeks at least Alice's landscape and mackerel drawings were replaced by cartoons and characters of well-known variety artistes; her friend and fellow artist, Jack Meredith was already making headlines with his caricature of performers on his pitch at Kingsway. Jack had been a stage actor for eight years, but unable to find work, he became a pavement artist to make a living. Jack and Alice had a lot in common – he was a fellow performer who had fallen on hard times and become a pavement artist to make ends meet.

The Music Hall Strike of 1907 took place between music hall employees, stage artistes and London theatre proprietors. Grievances in Edwardian England were as familiar as ours today: the catalyst for the strikes was employees' lack of pay, the scrapping of perks, an increase in working hours, and matinée performances.

The strike commenced on 22 January 1907 at the Holborn Empire and lasted for two weeks. The dispute gained momentum through support from popular entertainers including Marie Dainton, Marie Lloyd, Arthur Roberts, Joe Elvin and Gus Elen, all of whom were active on picket lines outside both London and provincial theatres.

The strikes ended two weeks later and resulted in a rise in pay and better working conditions for both stage workers

PAVEMENT ARTIST AND MUSIC-HALL STRIKE.

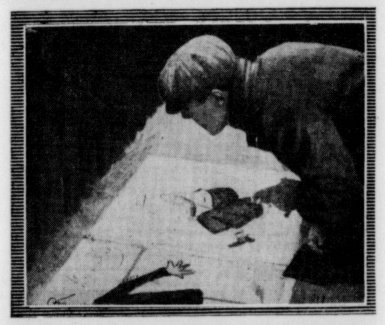

Crowds were attracted in the Kingsway yesterday by a pavement artist who hit on the novel idea of drawing artists engaged in the music-hall strike, including Little Tich and George Robey. — (*Daily Mirror* photograph.)

PRESS CUTTING: Jack Meredith at Kingsway, Daily Mirror, Saturday 9 February 1907

and artistes. The music hall and pavement art were closely related – both were performance art and both were considered crude and garish to the so called 'cultural elite' and arts establishments. Working-class 'folk art' was considered unworthy of recognition by the landed classes. The art of the poor, illiterate or down-at-heal did not figure within the hallowed halls of the Royal Academy. These were the salad days of the cultural elite; never before had the gulf between rich and poor been so great.

1907 Music Hall strike flyer

Artists would often be seen working the queues outside theatres.

Screevers knew how to 'play the crowd' and Music Hall stars were popular subjects for pavement pastellists; performers like Little Titch and Buffalo Bill always went down well. Popular actresses like Grace Hawthorne – whose image hung in the National Portrait Gallery – also graced the flagstones. Each pavement portrait would be accompanied by their name written underneath in perfect copperplate; or as Gus Elen so famously sang *"When he draws the king or czar, you can tell jist oo they are, by the writin' that is written underneath."*

Theatre critics – like this one from The Era – would often compere a poor theatrical performance with being *"as much like real life as the drawings of a pavement artist"* and *"with all the garish colour and artistic taste of a screever."*

But to call pavement art a performance art does the art form a disservice – in fact it straddles the line between both performance and visual. Producing art in a public place and attracting a large crowd of on-lookers is just like going on stage; the only difference is that a screever's performance evolves over many hours, rather than the typical 20 minutes or so of a street juggler or acrobat. For the artist, the feeling of nervousness before you 'perform' a new piece of work are very similar to the feelings of a stage performer. There was nowhere to hide on the pavement – no backstage area to gather your thoughts and cover up your mistakes; a street artist sinks or swims on raw talent, if you are found lacking, your audience will know.

CHAPTER FIVE

The Pavement Artist's Academy

In 1909, Alice took part in the *Pavement Artists Academy* competition. Screeving competitions had been reported before, but this was the first to document competitors and winners. It was organised by enlightened individuals, who recognised the value and artistry of screeving.

One of the competition judges was renowned Victorian and Edwardian illustrator Tom Browne; Browne is best known today for creating the Striding Man, a dapper Edwardian gentleman in mid-strut, created in 1908 for Johnnie Walker Scotch Whiskey.

The event took place at Fun City, Olympia, a kind of Edwardian amusement palace and the brainchild of English promoter Charles Blake Cochran. It was financed by a New

The Kensington Olympia, London c. 1886

York syndicate, and was predicted to 'make a fortune for its proprietors'. It was promoted as the Mammoth Fun City, reproducing the entertainments of Blackpool, Coney Island and the Parisian Expos. Among the attractions listed were a variety theatre, ballroom, continental circus, roller skating, and a miniature city inhabited by 100 midgets.

Also included were numerous mechanical rides, sideshows and spectacular re-enactments. Fun City was advertised across Britain as one of the main attractions for excursions to the Metropolis. No surprise then that the unusual sight of London screevers competing against each other should entertain and delight the Edwardian thrill seeker.

The competition was held in the annexe at Olympia on a Friday night – New Year's Day, 1909. For what was described as a novel competition for pavement artists, screevers were invited from all over the country to compete for prizes. Entries were received from Leeds, Glasgow, and Birmingham – not forgetting the most famous kerbstone artist in London, Lonely Jack, who had worked for 25 years at the corner of Baker Street and Marylebone Road. It gained national press attention, with the Daily Express reporting:

"Mrs. Colman, London's only woman pavement artist, is another celebrity who will compete."

There were also artists from Kensington High Street, and Notting Hill, whose respective artistic specialities were the vivid portrayal of two poached eggs resting on a rasher of bacon and shipwrecks. James Colman, Robert's brother and Alice's brother-in-law, also took part.

The competition judges were all illustrators: Lance Thackeray, William Nicholson, Tom Browne and John Hassall. All were commercial artists, illustrators and book designers – Browne, Thackeray and Hassall were founding members of the London Sketch Club, a social club for artists working in the field of commercial graphic art, and a club that is still going today. Hassall was primarily an illustrator, known for his advertisements and poster designs, while Nicholson was an English painter of still-life, landscapes and portraits. Also known for his work as a wood-engraver, illustrator, and author of children's books and designer for the theatre, Nicholson even did a self-portrait of himself as a pavement artist. All of the artists had at one time or another produced cartoons for Punch Magazine.

Tom Browne's Johnnie Walker illustration, 1908

The event started at 7pm prompt, and artists were given exactly one hour to complete their masterpieces... Judging commenced at 8pm, and prizes awarded accordingly. The same evening also featured a ladies' wrestling match, a piano-playing endurance competition and a beauty show.

This contemporary account of the evening's proceedings is taken from various sources, including the Daily Express, Manchester Courier and Lancashire General Advertiser, all on Saturday 2 January 1909.

Drawing seascapes and salmon against time

"A competition for the artists of the pavement; of the number that presented themselves only seven essayed to face the ordeal of working before the gaze of the assembled spectators.

"The pavement artists' Royal Academy had a brief but glorious career at the Fun City, Olympia, last night (1st Jan. 1909), with Mr Tom Browne, the artist, as judge and hanging committee. Crowds of people gathered round to see the artists at work. The time-limit was three-quarters of an hour, and money prizes were to be given to those who produced the best work.

"So with crayons and cardboard and canvas, the pavement painters sat them down. There was Albert Simpson, of Yarmouth, who learned the mastery and technique of the art as a distemper painter, and there was Arthur Harris, his arms tattooed tastefully with red rosebuds, known as the 'Pigeon Boy.' Because no man can draw a pigeon so skilfully as he, with the ring round its eye and the shimmer of green and purple on its feathers.

"Then there was Jim Hodges, who gave up home-decorating and now brightens the flagstones of Notting Hill. 'I can draw anything.' He said proudly, 'anywhere you like, in water-colour, on paper, in oil on cardboard.' Frederick Charles Warwick, the

Sargent of the streets, is the portrait specialist. Mrs Colman, the only woman competing, uses bath-brick on cardboard as the best medium to work with."

Lonely Jack's effort

And lastly there was Lonely Jack, who put more atmosphere into a fillet of salmon than any other artist – weather permitting.

'Go!' said the referee, and immediately there was a scraping of chalks and blurs of blue and yellow and red were smudged on the canvas. Lonely Jack drew two black lines very carefully, smudged them with the palm of his hand, and put in a yellow dot. 'An airship,' said a little girl to her brother. 'A torpedo,' the brother hazarded. Lonely Jack said nothing, but borrowed a piece of red chalk from the man next to him, who was drawing a Turner-esque sunset effect, and drew a red circle.

'A windmill', said a soldier. Lonely Jack smiled sadly, and went to work with blue. And lo! A salmon, neatly severed at the head, resulted. Jack screeved and scribbled. He put in green-edged shamrock. Having ignored yellow, hitherto, he added a lemon, and finally, in an orgy of art, he drew a white envelope, stamp, postage-mark, and all, and wrote on it 'Is my work worthy?'

Mr Tom Browne did not think so, for the prizes were awarded as follows:

First prize: Mrs Colman, for a landscape with two swans, called *Summer Landscape*

Second prize: Arthur Harris' evening landscape, entitled *Self-taught*, with a yellow butterfly and a cuckoo

Third prize: James Colman's Turner-esque seascape *Crossing the Channel by Moonlight*

Middlesex Music Hall Programme

"I like the atmosphere in the prize-winners' pictures," Tom Browne said. Lonely Jack was given a consolation prize.

"All of these artists were self-taught and their work showed some considerable merit. Miss Alice Geneviève Colman states that her ambition is to travel round the world, so that her work may get adequate recognition. Arthur Harris was formerly a cart-man, but left that occupation to follow his artistic bent, while another competitor, Simpson, of Yarmouth, said that he had never handled the chalks before. The spectators were keenly appreciative and it was well to know that all the competitors received some recompense for their efforts on this occasion," reported the Manchester Courier and Lancashire General Advertiser.

In competition, Alice completed no less than six sketches, whilst the men laboriously evolved one. She won £2 for her efforts – the equivalent of about £215 today.

Following her success at Fun City, Alice secured a week at The Old Middlesex Theatre in Drury Lane, as a Lightening Quick Sketch Artist. *The Old Mo* – as it was known – was a music hall, formally known as *The Mogul Saloon* and later *The Winter Gardens*. Today it is the site of The New London Theatre.

Alice appeared there, the very week a jury at the Old Bailey threw out a bill against a female artiste, Clementini Dolcini, who was charged with fatally shooting dead her assistant on stage, while he was playing the part of William Tell.

In its heyday, the theatre was described as 'not exactly the place to take a lady!', surrounded as it was by the Drury Lane gin palaces, open day and night. Only a few yards from the *Old Mo*, stood *The Coal Yard*, birthplace of Nell Gwynn, long-time mistress of King Charles II of England.

By 1911, Alice and family had moved to a tiny two roomed house at 48 Matilda Street in Islington. By this time her husband Robert was described as a 'scene painter' – probably casual work in and around London theatreland.

London pavement artists had a great sense of humour; when Leonardo da Vinci's masterpiece *The Mona Lisa* was stolen from the Louvre by an Italian painter and decorator on 21 August 1911, the screevers had a field day.

The very next day, every street artisan in London – including Alice – had made a reproduction of the Mona Lisa on the pavement, and – with varying degrees of enigmatic smile – had claimed theirs, in perfect copperplate lettering, to be *"the original masterpiece as once seen in The Louvre!"*

CHAPTER SIX

A Day with the Chalks

❧

In 1912, Alice wrote this fascinating account of her life as a pavement artist for Australia's Northern Star:

"My daily round (says Mrs Alice G. Colman, England's only lady pavement artist), unlike that of many people, is not always the same. Sometimes it consists of sitting disconsolately at home wondering if the skies will ever clear again; sometimes it consists of nothing but wandering through the streets of London, in search of a suitable pitch.

"There are over 300 male pavement artists in London, and most of them resent the intrusion of a woman into their ranks, so that time and time again I seek a favourite spot only to find huge initials chalked there. In the earlier days of my career I used to ignore these initials, and start work, but their owner invariably appeared and created a disturbance, so I have given up contesting my rights-the task is far too disagreeable.

"My husband (Robert) was a pavement artist long before I became one–though he really is a scene painter by trade, and in the days when we courted and married, against my grandmother's wishes, was a travelling acrobat. It was when he was badly ill, and starvation was staring us in the face, that I first went out armed with his own chalks and knelt with shaking limbs to decorate, the flagstones at Brook Green, Hammersmith.

"Fortunately, he is in better health now, and usually begins his daily round with mine. We breakfast at 9, and then, whatever the weather, so long as the pavements are dry, we set out– he, in one direction, I in another.

71

10513—28   LONDON LIFE.   A WOMAN PAVEMENT ARTIST. ROTARY PHOTO. E.C.
TO BE SEEN IN KINGSWAY. W.

Alice working at Kingsway, Rotary postcard, c.1912 (Photographer unknown)

"I carry my things in a little basket-my chalks, a mat to kneel on, a duster with which to obliterate the drawings at the end of the day, and a little metal plate in which to collect contributions.

"Having found a vacant spot that looks promising enough (on my unlucky days this doesn't happen till I have tramped about for hours), I take my mat from the basket, kneel upon it, and commence to draw.

"I reckon to finish three pictures in about ten minutes, but between each picture I rest for a while-partly to relieve my fingers, partly to give the crowd which always gathers round a chance to reward me for my pains.

"The crowd doesn't always reward me, but it asks the most extraordinary questions, and gives me the most curious advice. In spite of the fact that I am a wife and mother, I have received no less than 10 proposals of marriage out on the pavement!

"Usually I rub my 'gallery' out of existence at twilight and wind my way home, satisfied or dissatisfied according to the amount of my takings (I have taken as much as 5s 4d in a day, and-alas! how much more often-as little as nothing!) But if the pitch is a profitable one I occasionally stay on, working and exhibiting my work in the light of the electric arc lamp till 9 and even 10 o'clock.

"I have one meal-time during the day. Precisely at 2 o'clock I leave my pitch and my chalks to take care of themselves for half an hour, and resort to the nearest shop for something to eat.

"Most pavement artists desert their pitches in this way, and it is only at very rare intervals that any of the chalks are stolen or any of the pictures spoiled. But we are careful not to disappear till 2 o'clock strikes, and the children are safely in school!

Aches and pains

"Most people imagine that pavements are smooth, but, as a matter of fact, they are exceedingly rough; and, as I use my thumb and fingers, like different-sized paint-brushes, to tone and soften and spread the colours, I often go home with the blood oozing through the skin.

"That means a soaking in salt and water to harden them, and sometimes a wakeful night through the pain, but aches and pains are part and parcel of a pavement artist's life.

"Generally I am so tired when I get home that I am glad to go to bed, but on wet days, when my husband and I have been shut up indoors all day, we sometimes set off for the music-hall in the evening (if we can afford it). And there I study the scenery and the decorations quite as much as I do the performers, for one must always study even to be a woman pavement artist."

★★★★★

Her second surviving son, Robert Thomas Clyde Colman was born in Islington on 19 October 1912. Alice had become a real attraction at her pitch on Kingsway, and the Rotary Photographic Company even went so far as to produce a Rotograph Real Photograph postcard showing the female pavement artist at work.

Alice was 39 years of age in 1913, and some of the newspapers – this time the Manchester Courier and Lancashire General Advertiser, on 3 July 1913 – were not as complementary of Alice's demeanour as they had been in previous years...

"But there is just one profession which, so far as we know, no Mancunienne has yet adopted. This is the lucrative one of pavement artist – we dare hardly be correct and say artiste!

"In London this week, however, we discovered the first feminist capture of a pitch. The pioneer you may find on a sunny afternoon in Kingsway. But to be quite frank, she is disappointing.

"She is old not only in method and manner – but alas! – in years! There is nothing of Clements Inn* juvenility about this artist who draws so shabbily in its dapper shadow. She chalks no demand for votes – but merely for votive offerings.

"Her pictures are the old pictures – a wildly waving sea, a strangely sallow salmon, and ornate scrolls of appeal for help. Obviously the lady is a conservative in art. But like other artistic mandarins, she is successful; her copper-plate protestations are coining coppers."

*Clements Inn was the headquarters of the Women's Suffrage Movement. (WSPU)

In the winter, when the weather was too inclement for outdoor work, Alice started working for the Woman's Temperance Movement, assisting a well-known female temperance lecturer by providing rapid sketches illustrating her subject. It was a social movement against the consumption of alcoholic beverages, and promoting teetotalism; by 1913 it had developed a close allegiance to the women's suffrage movement.

Alice inspired many contemporary women to try pavement art as a career, but being in the wrong place at the wrong time could cost you dearly. There was the sad case of Lucy Askham, reported in the Evening Telegraph on 17 March 1913. Lucy was known as a pavement artist from Cambridge when her decapitated body was found in a ditch just outside Nuneaton. Two youths out for a walk with their dog made the grim discovery. The police reported that "There was a terrible gash on the right side of her neck, which had partially severed the head from the trunk." Lucy was about 40 years of age and single. It's uncertain if this crime was ever solved, but it underlines the dangers of being a female screever, working on the fringes of society.

CHAPTER SEVEN

World War I and Onwards

Men were taking the King's Shilling and war with Germany was declared on 28 July 1914. The only visible way in which the war affected the London pavement artist, beyond – to a certain extent – changing the character of their pictures, was in the matter of night exhibitions. Alice was known to have practiced pavement art by night, particularly during the summer months when artists could be seen working until midnight along the Thames. In Victorian England, screevers were a common sight on the streets of London and other major cities across Britain, with their work illuminated by candles or homemade oil lamps.

In his book of Christmas Stories in 1843, Charles Dickens wrote: *"Our conversation had brought us to a crowd of people, the greater part struggling for a front place from which to see something on the pavement, which proved to be various designs executed in coloured chalks on the pavement stones, lighted by two candles stuck in mud sconces."* In this description he is indeed talking about night screevers – pavement artists who took advantage of the short days and long nights leading up to Christmas.

The introduction of the new-fangled 'Arc Street Lamps' on the Embankment in 1881 saw it quickly became a favourite spot for night screevers who wished to save on the price of candles, and set themselves up under the shadow of free illuminations. There was a story of the night screever who discovered a lucrative pitch in Knightsbridge; he would appear at midnight and work through till dawn. The district was graced with one of the earliest-opening coffee stalls in the city, and early morning

World War I Zeppelin raid poster c.1916

trade was so brisk that the leather bag he used to carry his chalks in couldn't hold the pennies.

The long stretch of pavement between the top of Knightsbridge and Hyde Park Corner had become a profitable pitch for artists; they also enjoyed the fact that the pavements around there were paved with genuine York stone, that took the chalks well, rather than the inferior concrete pavements found in the less affluent areas of the city.

Robert's relapse

1914 was not a good year for Alice – only weeks before the outbreak of war, her husband Robert suffered a relapse of his old circus injuries and passed away at their home in Islington, on 1 July. He was 50. Robert was buried in an unmarked pauper's grave at Finchley Cemetery, North London. After more than 20 years of screeving – and the relative success and stability it had brought the Colman family, Alice was on her own again.

Later, Alice admitted to the Thompson Weekly News: "When my husband died I felt utterly alone in the world, I wondered what would happen to my two kiddies who were growing up."

To make ends meet, Alice took up a new pitch just down the road from Kingsway, on the long wide pavements at Aldwych. Her appearance attracted a great deal of attention. Even though Alice had been working the streets for many years, the sight of a woman pavement artist was still a novelty. Many tourists and people new to London had never seen such a thing. The culture of pavement art was unique to Britain and most particular London. She had taken to setting up early in the morning to attract the attention of the morning rush hour traffic. The stone was smooth and perfect for her landscape drawings. She would draw several of them, and at one end of the pictures chalked the following announcement in large beautiful copperplate letters:

77380 j.v.   PAVEMENT ARTIST   THAMES EMBANKMENT, LONDON
(BY NIGHT)

Night screeving on the Thames Embankment: postcard 1914

'A woman's endeavour to elucidate the abstruse problem of obtaining a livelihood.'

During the war, Alice had worked at a good many jobs; she was a nurse, a clerk, a canvasser and even a milkmaid. During World War I, women took on many roles traditionally done by men. In Liverpool, an entire army of women were employed to clean the streets while the men were away fighting. Alice worked as a kind of unofficial mid-wife – she had little or no training and was motivated solely by her socialist values. Health care was very thin on the ground and many working-class families found it difficult to afford professional help. But she always came back to the pavements..

Night screevers were a breed apart from their daytime cousins, although some, like Alice did work by both day and night, some chose only to work at night and their numbers were smaller. They were a sub culture within a subculture, and working by night was not without its dangers.

World War I saw the end of night screeving; it carried on until 1916, after which it was outlawed by blackout laws in London, following German Zeppelin air raids in 1915. The arc lights were extinguished at dusk, and it became illegal to even light candles. This unique culture of pavement art by night, which had existed for over 150 years in Britain was gone.

But the war also changed the demographic of Alice's patrons. During the daytime, she would take commissions for portraits and landscapes from American servicemen. After completing them in water colours at home, she would meet them back at her pitch to finalise the transaction.

The war ended on 11 November 1918, and by the following year the ranks of the pavement artist had more than tripled. Ex-soldiers, with their physical and mental scars, found it hard to gain employment ended up begging or eking a living as pavement artists. Attracting a little crowd at the side of the

Alice aged 40 and her son Robert Thomas Clyde, c.1914 (Colman family photo)

broad pavement spaces in Kingsway was a man with ribbons. His war medals were attached to a small piece of cardboard and propped up against the railings. The man was obviously very new to the work, for his drawings were crude even for a pavement artist.

He had scrawled on the pavement a notice to this effect: 'A member of the original Expeditionary Force to France; gassed and wounded at Ypres, suffering from a paralysed arm, discharged from the army, and unable to get work. Anyone interested may inspect my discharge papers.' The spectacle was a depressing one; on seeing this, a female passer-by started volubly declaiming against the Government and the War Office for allowing such a thing. Another pavement artist near Euston Station proclaimed that he had been 'severely wounded during the retreat from Mons'. Another pavement artist with ribbons, whose favourite spot was near Charing Cross railway bridge, decorated the flagstones neatly and accurately with famous army divisional badges worn by the troops in France. They made an attractive collection and appealed to the ex-serviceman who may have felt generous towards his old badge.

During the war, a number of women had, for a short time at least, joined the craft of screever, usually on the plea of 'children to support through a husband having been killed in the war'. There were no war pensions, and disabled ex-serviceman with no means of support were forced to become pedlars and street artists. It was a humiliation to the nation, to say nothing of its effect on the men themselves.

The debate became known as 'the Pensions Question' and following the political embarrassment of so many injured service men being discharged and forced to work on the streets as pavement artists and beggars; in 1916 a Parliamentary Select Committee recommended that the existing pension provisions should be incorporated into one War Pension Scheme administered by a new department. In 1917 the Ministry of

---

A HEART CRY.

In the Strand to-day, just where the Kingsway palaces of commerce avenue towards Holborn, I came upon a pavement artist's pitch. The artist, evidently a woman, was not visible. But her gallery of crayon drawings was there, including a wistful one of a Nun, with crossed hands over a rosary, and a delicate stained-glass background, which may have been an artistic expression of secret personal yearnings to be at rest out of the unkind London hurly-burly.

But what struck me was the chalk writing, in a cultured woman's hand, beside the drawings, " An attempt to elucidate the domestic problem!" Some tragedy here, I fancy. But I could not find the artist.

Cutting from the Nottingham Evening Post, 1 November 1924

Pensions was established, later becoming the Department of Social Security. Although this didn't completely solve the problem, it eventually led to the establishment of a living War Pension for ex-servicemen and a social security benefits system for the unemployed in Britain.

If you want to take to pulse of a nation, then you only have to look at its streets. In Britain everything happened on the streets. Whole galaxies of the arts and artists overlooked by the establishment; practitioners never invited to exhibit or play a part in the future of art, and yet they exist regardless of the establishment. The illegitimate muses and half-sisters of the art world did their best in all weathers to brighten the streets of London, and in turn the lives of the people who walk them. Earnest, sad-eyed old men devoted their lives to decorating the flagstones, holding up a mirror to society on every street corner on every day.

★★★★★

Alice married her second husband, Walter Henry Oxley on Wednesday 10 August 1921; he was a signwriter and gilder and ten years older than Alice, who was now 47. They lived at 33 Wilton Square, North London. It's likely that Walter was a family friend of Alice's first husband Robert – at one time he even lived in the same street as the Colman family. Being a signwriter, he would have made friends easily with fellow creatives Alice and Robert.

"Some days you may sit eight or ten hours and only pick up a few coppers," Alice told the Hull Daily Mail, as she returned to her old pitch on the Victoria Embankment, outside King's College. The year was 1933 and Alice was 59; it was while putting the finishing touches to a landscape that she was approached by a journalist from the Thompson Weekly News, who asked her about her life on the street as England's only female pavement artist. Alice was still enthusiastic "I like life!" she said, and added "You must keep cheerful if you want to make a success as a pavement artist."

PRESS CUTTING: 1933: Alice Geneviève Oxley (Colman), aged 60

Alice Oxley (Colman) with her cousin Albert Shattock: c.1921
(Colman family photo). Alice still harboured ambition for theatrical performance,
and was photographed in costume for an unknown production with her cousin
and actor Albert Shattock.

Alice had been entertaining people on the streets for over 41 years. She enjoyed the open air life, and was quite satisfied with the pecuniary results. In all those years, her only absence was due to bad weather, rain or snow, or during the short periods of casual work she took to make both ends meet. "Why do I still keep to my chalks? Well, we are still having a little hard luck, and, anyway, I like them too much now to give them up," she told him.

Alice did the newspaper interview with the journalist who had sought her out on the Victoria Embankment, and it was published in the Thomson Weekly News, on Saturday 29 July 1933.

The woman who smiled through years of sorrow

"Meet Alice Oxley (Colman), the only woman pavement artist in London. A smiling old lady of sixty, she has been on her pitch by the Embankment for thirty years, and everyone calls her the 'Smiling artist'.

"But few who toss pennies into her little tray knew what tragedy lay behind her smile, or why she first took to her chalks. It all happened soon after her happy wedding to a trapeze artiste. Two bonnie little children, a girl and boy, were born, and life seemed just a happy dream to the young couple.

"Then, one day, as he was performing at the circus, the young man fell from the dizzy height of the 'big top' into the sawdust ring, and became a helpless cripple for the rest of his life.

"They brought him home on a stretcher, with his circus paint still on his face. They told his young wife that he would never be able to work again.

"From that day their whole outlook changed. Their savings dwindled every day until only a few shillings remained, while he lay on his bed unable to raise a finger to help the little family. Mrs Oxley knew no trade to which she could turn, and her only hobby before her marriage had been drawing.

"So, putting her pride in her pocket, she went to a district where she was not known, she drew her pictures on the pavement. In that way she earned enough to keep the wolf from the door.

"Her husband lay between life and death for over a year. Then he began to mend slowly, until at last he was able to walk with help, but still he had to depend on his stout little wife. Every day she went out with her coloured chalks, trying to earn a few shillings.

Best Husband in the World

"Then her husband had a relapse and died, leaving her and her kiddies with nothing to keep them. Mrs. Oxley told her story to a *Thomson's Weekly News* representative, while she drew her pictures on the pavement. 'There is no use worrying over anything, I have found,' she said, 'and although I have had a very hard life I try to keep smiling whatever happens.

"'I was very happy when I married, and my husband was the best husband in the world. We had saved quite a nice little nest egg in case anything happened, but we never thought that we would want it so soon.

"'After my husband's accident I tried to get work, but could find nothing.

"'As my hobby had been drawing, the idea came to me that I might be able to earn enough to keep us all by being a woman pavement artist.

"'With the last of our savings I bought some chalks, and in a nearby district where I was unknown, I drew my first sketches.

Downhearted

"'Sometimes I felt downhearted when the rain came and washed away a morning's work, but I soon learned that it is no use crying over a spoilt drawing or two. Sometimes, on the other hand, I felt that I would like to take away a flagstone after I had drawn a particularly good one, for I love pretty colours.

"'When my husband died I felt utterly alone in the world, I wondered what would happen to my two kiddies who were growing up.

"'My pitch along by the Embankment was chosen because, when my husband was alive, it used to be his favourite walk.

"'My two kiddies, I still call them kiddies, have grown up now. The girl is happily married and the boy has grown to a fine young man. Although it was a struggle to bring them up, the result has been the best reward that I could hope for.

"'A long time after my husband's death I married again, and we are very happy.

"'Why do I still keep to my chalks? Well, we are still having a little hard luck, and, anyway, I like them too much now to give them up.'"

★★★★★

Just three days later, on the Tuesday evening, Alice returned home and ran a bath, complaining of feeling a little unwell and under the weather.

The following day, Alice Geneviève Oxley died of heart failure and acute bronchitis at her home in Islington, on the last day of January, 1934. She was aged 60. She was buried in an unmarked grave, number 22500, section M, at Islington Cemetery, East Finchley, the same cemetery as her late beloved husband Robert.

IN LOVING MEMORY

of

Alice Genevieve Oxley,

WHO PASSED AWAY JANUARY 31st, 1934.

AGED 60 YEARS

Laid to rest at Islington Cemetery, East Finchley
Church Ground Grave No. 22500 Section M.

Alice's funeral memorial card 1934 (Colman family archive)

"And so, after an arduous day's work and with the daylight failing, Mrs Colman cleans off her pitch and makes her way home," the London Evening Post lamented.

Like all pavement artists, her name was forgotten, and her work was considered too lowly to record. As ephemeral as the work she created on the pavements, to date no known examples of Alice's work have been found.

Alice's studio was large and airy, and – except on foggy days – was well lit and rent free. The flagstones were nice, square and smooth; kneeling on the pavement with a good heart, she gave scope to her creative expression in an age when free speech and creativity for women was extraordinarily rare. The freedom to express and create not only made Alice a living to support her family, but made her feel good: it removed the shackles and drudgery of everyday life. It made her feel good about herself and the world around her. From the moment she purchased her first chalks, it was a personal journey of discovery. Alice's real gift was to share that spirit with the world.

So what of Alice's two children?

Well by all accounts, Alice did a good job; seven months after his mother's death Robert got married to Leonora Margaret Clare, in Stoke Newington on 22 August 1934. They had two children, and Robert served as a Corporal in the Royal Marines during World War II. He was also a very talented amateur artist. He died at Edgware in 1971 aged 59.

Alice's daughter Maud Dorothy went on to become a nurse. She married Frederick John Dodman on 16 May 1911; they had two children together (Fred and Dorothy) but sadly her husband Fred died in action in France during World War I, aged 32. Alice herself did a number of other jobs during the war, and – following the death of Frederick – would have found herself under extra pressure to again support her daughter and grandchildren.

Alice's son Robert on his wedding day in 1934 (Colman family photo)

Maud married for a second time on 26 August 1919, to Alfred Alsop Hillman; together they had six children (Phyllis, Henry, Ron, Colin, Tony and Pam).

★★★★★

The events which affect us most in life generally happen quietly – when we are engaged in our daily work, and thinking least about them. The transformation of a single lowly flagstone into a beautiful and 'valuable' work of art is simple and magical. Like butterflies on a summer's day, a fleeting glimpse into another world, a child's memory of jumping into pavement paintings. To marvel at the artists skill and imagination, and effectively say; there must be more to life than this!

Pavement artists create all of these things and more, curving time and space. By creating art in a public place they enter into a 'zone' where time slows down – they are in a different physical reality than the people who observe the art. If you take the time to look, the atmosphere on a once drab, uninteresting street, in the middle of a big city becomes transformed into a relaxed and friendly place to be – strangers start talking to each other and children start laughing and magic is unleashed.

Pamela Travers, the writer of Mary Poppins once remarked that if you scratch beneath the surface of everyday life, you will find magic. Street art was brought to life and beamed into millions of imaginations when the 1964 release of Disney's Mary Poppins introduced Bert the screever to a new generation.

Pavement art is a kind of magical performance art within its own time zone. Not the instant fix of the street musician or clown juggler. The pavement artist's 'show' becomes like a string of pearls cast at the feet of the flagstone traveller. Art that is given away freely – yours to take from if you wish, no charge, but if you'd like to drop a few coppers in the hat or tin tray, then that's OK too.

When I started my research into pavement art, I had no idea Alice even existed, but I'm glad she did. Innovation and progress usually starts with individuals doing what seem to be small but extraordinary things. I am delighted to have found Alice, and presented her story to you here for the first time.

Only a few years earlier, Jack the Ripper was stalking the streets around Whitechapel. Women didn't have the right to vote, the industrial revolution was still in full flow and London had become the biggest and richest metropolis the world had ever seen. It was a time when women 'knew their place' and children were 'seen and not heard.' Alice emerged from the fog strewn streets of old London town, like some long-forgotten character in Walt Disney's Mary Poppins; jumping in and out of chalk pavement drawings to enthral and delight us with her own brand of street magic.

Indeed, it is not too fanciful an idea to imagine that Pamela Travers had stumbled upon Alice when she arrived in England in 1924 and based her famous creation on this most unusual of screevers.

Few people can truly be considered the first or a pioneer in their field, but Alice Colman is one of those rare individuals who paved the way and saw the future for pavement art. Not just to be considered a 'beggars art' but as a serious art form within its own right. Alice was London's first professional female pavement artist.

Looking back on her career, Alice told the Thompson Weekly News in 1933: "As my hobby had been drawing, the idea came to me that I might be able to earn enough to keep us all by being a woman pavement artist."

Pavement art now

Over the last 50 years, the changes in pavement art have been seismic.

We now have a worldwide arts movement that has given birth to a myriad of festivals and events dedicated solely to street chalking art. Mexico, the USA, Italy, Australia, Netherlands, France and Germany all hold annual street painting festivals. Disney's Mary Poppins was released in 1964, and a whole generation of children discovered Bert the screever.

Street art festivals like the Bella-Via in Mexico, the Toulon Chalking Festival in France and the Sarasota Chalk Festival in the USA, (all organised by women) continue to inspire new and fresh artistic talent...

Female pavement artists can be found right across the globe. They continue to innovate and move the art form in all kinds of new directions. They have dynamic and interesting ideas for involving people in the creative process. I hope that this book will provide an inspiration to anybody who wishes to create or appreciate live art on the public pavement stage.

Today it's cool to be a female pavement artist: Portsmouth 2007
(photo: Catherine McMahon)

CHAPTER EIGHT

Appendix

I n keeping with many pavement artists, Alice led a double life; she courted the press and gained celebrity status on one hand, whilst on the other she kept her activities on the street a complete secret to all but her immediate family.

So when I contacted Alice's grandson Robert about the writing of this book, he knew almost nothing about her life as a pavement artist. It all came as a big surprise. I interviewed Robert in 2013, at his home in Bedford. He supplied me with family photos and memorabilia that provided a useful insight to Alice's personal life.

Alice's grandson Robert with his wife Ruth at their home in Bedford
(Photo: Philip Battle)

Interview with Robert Colman (Alice's grandson) 5 October 2013

What can you tell me about Alice's early life?

We have never found a birth certificate for Alice, so we know very little about her childhood, other than the fact that she put her father as being Noel Temple on her marriage certificate. He was an actor and playwright apparently.

There was a story that Alice was adopted; was Noel Temple, as it says on the marriage certificate, her father? This was word of mouth family history as passed down to us, but we don't know if it's true.

My side of the family were told that Alice's mother, my great grandmother, was an opera singer and that she had a dalliance with a Spanish Count – they got married, and Alice was the result. The Count's family hotfooted it to England and the marriage was annulled and the Count and his family returned to Spain.

There was another family story going a long way back; we were told that it was an Italian Marquis, but the rest of the story was the same. A large sum of money was put into a trust fund for Alice somewhere along the way, and a solicitor ran off with all the money. That's the story; don't know how true it is!

What did you know about Alice's life as a pavement artist?

As a family, we didn't know a great deal about her pavement artist days. To us, and what we knew, it only played a small part – it didn't seem very important to us. We certainly didn't know about all this newspaper coverage – we've got nothing like this; it has come as a complete revelation.

Alice was very secretive about her work as a pavement artist, she never said very much about what she did; she hated people and family recognising her when she was either working or travelling to and fro from her 'business'. My mum Nora, (Leonora Margaret Clare) – Alice's daughter-in-law – said that when she was engaged to my father, she got on a bus in north London, going to Edgware, and Alice was sitting on the bus upstairs. My mother went to say hello and Alice was waving her arms at her as much as if to say don't come near me, you don't know me! My mother had got on the bus at Burnt Oak to visit my father's sister my Aunt Maud (Maud Dorothy Colman) and clearly Alice was going there also.

My Aunt Maud once told me that Alice sometimes did her chalk drawings outside the Co-op at Burnt Oak and if any of the family came upon her she would ignore them. Perhaps that is what she had been doing when my mum met her!

We were told that Alice used to work regularly at the Chelsea Embankment; there were a lot of people with money around there.

Did you know that Alice appeared at Olympia?

We didn't know that she had won a prize in pavement art at Olympia – I can't even remember my father saying that, but he did tell me once, a few years before he died, that his mum was in all the newspapers and they were saying *"who was this mysterious woman, where did she come from?"* It was like she was living a double life.

Can you tell me about your grandfather, Alice's first husband Robert?

Robert (my grandfather) had several brothers, and from what I've heard the three brothers made an act, an acrobatic act.

My brother Colin remembers that they were called 'The Jumping Jacks' – apparently one of their specialities was to jump over something, on to some eggs, without breaking them.

Robert (my dad) never knew his father at all. He was born in 1912 and his dad died in 1914. But he was told by his sister – my Aunt Maud – that his dad used to play with him and bounce him on his knee so he obviously loved him. He was thrilled when my dad was born.

My impression was that Robert had been partially paralysed due to his fall in the circus. I was told a story, that before his accident, Robert was walking through London Town and he stopped this fellow beating up a dog in the street with a stick. He remonstrated with him, but the man would not stop so he wrestled the stick from his hands and a fight broke out. A crowd gathered and started making bets as to who would win. They all bet on the short fella, the little fella, because Robert was a little guy, and of course Robert won and the whole crowd cheered. It is nice to think he would do such a thing; he was that kind of fella, to stop somebody being cruel to a dog.

What about Alice's children?

Alice had between four and six children as far as we know but only two survived. Maud was the eldest, then Alice, who died of consumption. Ethel who swallowed a coin and got gangrene and then there was Robert; the middle two girls had both died before my father Robert was born.

Do you know if Alice was ever involved in the Suffragette movement?

I don't think Alice was involved with the Suffragettes, but she did have strong views – she had her head screwed on, that's for sure. Towards the end of her life in the 1930s, she was walking through central London when she saw some of Oswald Mosley's

Blackshirts (British Union of Fascists) protesting and marching down the street, handing out fascist leaflets. One of them handed one to Alice and she hit him with her handbag!

Do you have any family oral history stories about Alice?

My dad told me once that Grandma Colman was walking down the street, when this rider-less horse came galloping down. Everybody was running for their lives shouting and everything – she went into the middle of the road, stuck her arms out and closed her eyes... the horse went round her and carried on. He was laughing, he couldn't believe that the horse went round her.

My mum said that Alice had very dark black eyes and if she got angry she would 'flash her eyes' and you could tell she was annoyed!

She also said that Alice and her son would sometimes start dancing together, clicking their fingers and arms in the air, Robert with a rose in his teeth dancing in a Spanish gypsy style.

One day Alice discovered her son playing with a toy gun he had found in the street. She took the gun off him and threw it in the canal, as if to say, 'don't play with guns!'

Alice's second husband (Walter Henry Oxley) used to drink, and my father Robert, Alice's son, didn't get on with him; one day they had an argument and Oxley hit him and knocked him right down the stairs, and he broke his collarbone.

My aunt's cousin Emily used to use shoe polish to blacken her hair – it was a common thing to do back then. She was quite eccentric though, I think she got it from Alice.

My dad used to say to my mum that if anything went wrong, and we couldn't pay our way, he could always go out on the street and draw. He was always good at art, I think he got that from his mum, Alice.

What do you know about Alice during the First World War?

When our families meet up, it's good comparing notes on what we were told about our grandparents or great grandparents. My mother remembers stories of my grandmother Alice, in World War I, running down into the underground, going into one of those tunnels to avoid the bombs coming down from one of these airships – a German Zeppelin by all accounts. She would take my dad into the railway tunnels, probably the local underground, to escape the bombings. I would imagine this was either late 1916 or 1917.

Another thing I was told that during the War, she was getting commissions for portraits and pictures from American service men on the street, she did them in water colours at home, met them back at her pitch, and they would give her money to take back home, I don't know how true this was but it makes sense.

What about Alice in later life?

In later years, Alice became well known for helping distressed women in childbirth, like an unofficial midwife. My dad remembers people calling at the door and asking for her help. People did not have much money to send for a doctor or proper midwife back then.

The sad part of it is that Alice was buried in a pauper's grave in Finchley, North London, the Islington cemetery. I have been up and found the general area but it's all grass and bushes and unmarked. The same with her husband Robert – he's buried in the same cemetery, a few rows up and further back, unmarked again. The two of them are there, it's sad!

My brother and I thought about getting them exhumed; I have got the grave numbers and plans but how would you know who was who? They were public graves and they are buried with a lot of strangers.

Alice's known pavement art pitches

Some of the known and documented places Alice used as 'pitches' to produce pavement art:

- 1893: Brook Green, Hammersmith, London
  (Source: The London Evening Post – Wed 24 Sept 1913)

- 1893: Grays Inn Road, London
  (Source: Grantham Journal – 14 October 1893)

- 1893: St. John's Wood, London
  (Source: The Lloyds Weekly 1893)

- 1894: Pentonville Hill, London
  (Source: Albury Banner – 16 April 1909)

- 1896: Kensington, London
  (Source: Yorkshire Evening Post – 16 April 1896)

- 1897: St Martin-in-the-Field Church, London
  (Source: The Westminster Budget – 8 October 1897)

- 1898: The Royal Academy, Bloomsbury, London
  (Source: The English Illustrated Magazine – October 1898)

- 1899: Victoria Embankment- Between Waterloo & Westminster Bridge
  (Source: Lloyds Weekly Newspaper – 30 July 1899)

- 1899: Queen Anne's Mansions, beside St James's Park
  (Source: Edinburgh Evening News – 6 May 1899)

- 1899: Bridge Street, Leighton Buzzard
  (Source: Leighton Buzzard Observer and Linslade Gazette – 12 September 1899)

- 1903: Outside the British Museum
  (Source: The London Daily News – 12 December 1903)

POSTCARD: Grays Inn Road, London Cir.1930

POSTCARD: St. John's Wood Cir.1900

- 1906: Holborn end of Kingsway; right hand side, coming towards The Strand,
  (Source: Daily Express – 23 August 1906)

- 1907: Marble Arch, London
  (Source: Portsmouth Evening News – 13 February 1907)

- 1921: Aldwych, London
  (Source: Derby Daily Telegraph – 27 January 1921)

- 1922: The Strand, London
  (Source: The Hartlepool Mail – 11 January 1922)

- 1933: Victoria Embankment, London
  (Source: Hull Daily Mail – 27 July 1933)

POSTCARD: Victoria Embankment Cir. 1890

Alice's known homes and residences

Some of the places Alice actually lived between 1873 and 1934.

- 1873/4: Birth – Paddington, London
  (Source: Marriage certificate between Alice Temple and Robert Colman)

- 1891: 30 November (Age 18) – 3 Branston Street, Kensington
  (Source: Certificate, Marriage to Robert Colman)

- 1894: 13 March (Age 20) – 73 Latymer Road, Hammersmith
  (Source: Baptism of daughter Maud Dorothy Colman)

- 1900: 27 March (Age 26) – 8 Bransford Street, Kensington
  (Source: Baptism of daughter Ethel Mary Colman)

- 1911: (Age 38) – 48 Matilda Street, Islington
  (Source: 1911 census)

- 1914: 1 July (Age 40) – 4 Henry Place, Islington
  (Source: death certificate of husband, Robert Colman)

- 1918: 269, New North Road, Islington
  (Source: London Electoral Registers, 1832-1965)

- 1921: 10 August (Age 48) – 33 Wilton Square, Islington
  (Source: marriage certificate of Alice G Colman to Walter Oxley)

- 1922: 267 New North Road, Islington
  (Source: London Electoral Registers, 1832-1965)

- 1926 to 1934: 40 St Paul Street, Islington
  (Source: London Electoral Registers, 1832-1965)

POSTCARD: Kensington High Street 1890

POSTCARD: Islington 1919

POSTCARD: Islington High Street 1930s

PAVEMENT ARTIST

Also known as *street artist:* This is an overall term to describe any person creating art on the pavement in a public place. This is not limited to chalking art but can include all art forms. In the late 1800s, street potters, paper cutters and so-called 'writers without hands' were also classed as pavement artists.

SCREEVER

A British slang term for pavement artist; this relates to artists working directly on the pavement with chalks. The term harks back to how street art developed in Britain and Ireland, the word screever (Scrivener/Scribe) is thought to originate in Elizabethan England and is based on the written words and messages that became known as *begging letters, the copperplate lettering* that artists performed on the street. Eventually the term was used to describe all artists working in chalks on the pavement.

In Henry Mayhew's *London Labour and the Poor;* 1851 *(a Cyclopaedia of the Condition and Earnings of those that will work, those that cannot work, and those that will not work)*, pavement artists were classed in Vol. 1 *The London Street Folk* as: 'The Street-Artists – as black profile-cutters, blind paper-cutters "screevers", or draughtsmen in coloured chalk on the pavement, writers without hands, and readers without eyes.'

CHALKS

Drawing material used by pavement artists, primarily because they would easily wash away with the rain and not damage the pavements. Pavement art was tolerated in Britain, providing the artist washed away their work at the end of each day. To save money, many artists made their own chalks at home, a tradition that goes back hundreds of years. George Orwell, in his 1933 novel, *Down and out in Paris and London,* describes a chalk recipe made by London pavement artists, as consisting of coloured pigments and condensed milk!

Before chalks, artists would use broken bits of clay smoking pipes to 'screeve' messages and artwork on the pavement.

PITCH

This would be a location were a pavement artist would set-up chalking the pavement. Many prime pitches would be highly prized, and often turf wars could arise by opportunists, setting up on a lucrative pitch. Fights were not uncommon. In London, some 'old timers' worked the same pitches for over 40 years.

BOARD MEN

A pavement artist who produces all his works on boards or canvas; a *board man* does not work directly onto the pavement, but onto canvas, boards or paper. This method may be more flexible when it comes to being 'moved on.'

Sometimes screevers would bring along pre-prepared drawings and paintings on boards to sell to passers-by. Board men were not considered real pavement artists by traditional screevers, because much of the work produced was done at home, or even by another artist and many board men were looked up on as being 'no better than beggars.'

CADGER SCREEVERS

An old term for pavement artists who couldn't really draw, and pretended to be artists. Some cadgers used to pay real artists to hire out pictures for the day, and beg for money on the pavement without doing any art. This old scam was well known and generally hated by the genuine pavement artist, as it gave everybody a bad name.

If caught begging by the police, a cadger screever was often asked to prove his 'artistry' before a judge, who would produce a piece of paper and chalks for the defendant to draw on in court. They were soon found out!

STREET PAINTER

A modern day term to describe a pavement artist; street painters today use a mixture of chalks, pastels and water-based paints or pure pigments to decorate the streets. The term is only very recent (within the last ten years) and originates from the pavement art festivals movement.

MADONNARI

A term used to describe Italian street painters; following the tradition of pavement artists painting /chalking the Madonna and child on the pavement. The term is thought to date back to the 1500s but firm evidence of this is not yet proven. It seems the modern tradition of Italian Street Painting began in the mid 1970s with a number of festivals and events in Italy and the USA. The Madonnari artists use chalks directly on the pavement, mainly producing art based upon a Catholic Religious theme.

ABOUT THE AUTHOR

Philip Battle

I was born in Prescot, Lancashire in 1958 and brought up by my grandmother Eleanor Rigby. 1962 was my defining year – when my mother had had enough and abandoned me and my two siblings at a bus shelter in Salford, Manchester, my life suddenly became 'special' and I had a story to tell.

I have always wanted to write; I wrote my first book of poems *A Sky Full of Secrets* back in 1978, but I was never brave enough to publish it. Writing books and stuff is not the done thing when you're the product of a broken home, semi-literate and suffering from appallingly low self-esteem. In 1981 I became a writer and designer for *Breakout* music and arts fanzine in Liverpool. The following year I formed my own band and started my ill-fated career as a live performance poet. I was in good company; Julian

Cope once asked me to be in his band (*Teardrop Explodes*) and I was at the centre of the early '80s music boom in Liverpool; a good place to be in my opinion!

I decided to make a career as an artist and sallied forth into the world of art and graphic design. I spent a brief period as an illustration tutor at The University of Liverpool before becoming a supervisor in adult education. I've spent the past 20 years of my life travelling the world as a professional pavement artist. This book represents my third, but is the first to be published on the subject of this much misunderstood art-form.

Me as a person

I'm a compulsive communicator who needs to say stuff even if it means talking to myself all day. I'm a phone-a-phobic who believes it's healthy to have a dialogue with oneself.

I've lived my entire life trying to make sense of it all, and, the truth is, as the song goes, 'The further one travels the less one knows'.

I live with my partner Catherine and a cat called Rosie, in Liverpool, UK – the creative centre of the universe.

We run a company called UrbanCanvas – www.urbancanvas. org.uk – providing visual street art projects for festivals and events.

If you have any comments, suggestions or views about this publication then I would love to hear from you. You can email me directly at urbancanvas@live.co.uk.

PHOTO CREDITS AND REFERENCES

Page 2: The Lady Pavement Artist: Nottinghamshire Guardian, 21 October 1893. Image © THE BRITISH LIBRARY BOARD. ALL RIGHTS RESERVED.

Page 3: Alice Geneviève Temple, age 17 c.1890 © The Colman family archive, 2015

Page 5: Alice Geneviève Temple (second from left), age 17 c.1890 © The Colman family archive, 2015

Page 6: Street Acrobats: The Graphic magazine, 1890. Image © THE BRITISH LIBRARY BOARD. ALL RIGHTS RESERVED.

Page 11: Press cutting, Yorkshire Weekly Post, 21 October 1893. Image © THE BRITISH LIBRARY BOARD. ALL RIGHTS RESERVED.

Page 12: Alice G. Colman, The Lady Pavement Artist, 1893. Illustrated by Lionel J Jones Image © THE BRITISH LIBRARY BOARD. ALL RIGHTS RESERVED.

Page 13: The home of Alice Colman, 73 Latymer Road, Hammersmith. Westminster Budget, December 1893. Illustrated by Lionel J Jones Image © THE BRITISH LIBRARY BOARD. ALL RIGHTS RESERVED.

Page 14: Press cutting. Sheffield Daily Telegraph, 12 October 1893. Image © THE BRITISH LIBRARY BOARD. ALL RIGHTS RESERVED.

Page 15: Alice's daughter Maud Dorothy's baptism. 3 April 1894. Image © London Metropolitan Archives

Page 17: Press cutting, Daily Gazette for Middlesbrough, 23 September 1896. Image © THE BRITISH LIBRARY BOARD. ALL RIGHTS RESERVED.

Page 18: English stage actress Beatrice Stella Tanner (Mrs. Patrick Campbell) © Unknown

Page 23: Alice Colman as described in the Westminster Budget © Public domain

Page 27: Press cutting, Gloucester Citizen. Image © THE BRITISH LIBRARY BOARD. ALL RIGHTS RESERVED.

Page 32: Alice Colman on Victoria Embankment, Lloyds Weekly Newspaper, 30 July 1899. Image © THE BRITISH LIBRARY BOARD. ALL RIGHTS RESERVED.

Page 35: Alice on the Thames Embankment, Leeds Times, 5 August 1899. Image © THE BRITISH LIBRARY BOARD. ALL RIGHTS RESERVED.

Page 43: 1901 Census: Alice and Robert Colman © Crown Copyright Image, reproduced by courtesy of The National Archives, London England

Page 43: Alice postcard, published by Cassell, 1901 © Public domain

Page 45: Alice, the lady pavement artist. Press cutting, Daily Mirror, 15 November 1906. Image © Daily Mirror Newspapers

Page 46: Alice Colman at her pitch in Kingsway, London, age 32. Published in The Sketch, 1906. Image © Philip Battle Collection

Page 47: Press cutting, Manchester Courier and Lancashire General Advertiser, 22 August 1906. Image ©THE BRITISH LIBRARY BOARD. ALL RIGHTS RESERVED.

Page 49: This is the house that man built: Suffragette postcard c.1910 ©Public domain

Page 51: Press cutting, Daily Express, 23 August 1906. Image © Express Newspapers N&S Syndication

Page 51: Postcard in the Suffragette colours of green, white and purple, c.1907 ©Public domain

Page 52: Suffragette pavement artists, 1913. © Public domain

Page 52: Suffragette pavement artists, 1913 © Crown Copyright Image, reproduced by courtesy of The National Archives, London England

Page 54: Glass lantern slide: an artist working along the Thames Embankment c.1900 © Philip Battle collection

Page 55: Screevers attracted large crowds – glass lantern slide of George Blaber at his pitch in Nottingham c.1906 © Philip Battle collection

Page 56: Pavement artist James Carling in Liverpool, c.1869, courtesy of the Carling Family Archive

Page 59: Jack Meredith at Kingsway, Daily Mirror, 9 February 1907. Image © Daily Mirror Newspapers

Page 60: 1907 Music Hall strike flyer © Public domain

Page 63: The Kensington Olympia, London c.1886. © Public domain

Page 65: Tom Browne's Johnnie Walker illustration, 1908 © Public domain

Page 68: Middlesex Music Hall Programme, © Public domain

Page 72: Alice working at Kingsway, Rotary Postcard, c.1912. Photo © Philip Battle Collection 2015

Page 78: World War I Zeppelin raid poster, c. 1916 © Public domain

Page 80: Night screeving on the Thames Embankment, postcard 1914. Photo © Philip Battle Collection

Page 81: Alice and her son Robert Thomas Clyde, 1914. © The Colman family archive, 2015

Page 83: Cutting from the Nottingham Evening Post, 1 November 1924 ©THE BRITISH LIBRARY BOARD. ALL RIGHTS RESERVED.

Page 84: Thomson Weekly News, 1933. Published by kind permission of D C Thomson & Co Ltd, Dundee

Page 85: Alice Oxley Colman with her cousin Albert Shattock, 1921 ©The Colman family archive, 2015

Page 89: Alice's funeral memorial card, 1934 © The Colman family archive, 2015

Page 90: Alice's son Robert on the day of his wedding, 1934 © The Colman family archive, 2015

Page 93: Today it's cool to be a female pavement artist. Portsmouth, 2007. Photo by Catherine McMahon © UrbanCanvas 2007

Page 95: Alice's grandson Robert with his wife Ruth at their home in Bedford, 2013. Photo by Philip Battle. © Philip Battle 2015

Page 103: Gray's Inn Road, London postcard, c.1930 © Public domain

Page 103: St. John's Wood postcard, c.1900 © Public domain

Page 104: Victoria Embankment postcard, c.1890 © Public domain

Page 106: Kensington High Street postcard, 1890 © Public domain

Page 106: Islington postcard, 1919 © Public domain

Page 107: Islington High Street postcard, 1930s © Public domain

Page 108: World News Sydney, 4 October 1913 © Public domain

Page 113: Philip Battle © 2015

Historical sources:

Ancestry.co.uk

The Colman family archive

The British Newspaper Archive

The General Register Office

UK Press Online

National Archives

The New York Times

TROVE - National Library of Australia

The London Book by Francis Marshall

Every effort has been made to fulfil requirements with regard to reproducing copyright material. The publisher will be glad to rectify any omissions at the earliest opportunity.